Cover: **Homework**
by Winslow Homer (1836-1910)
watercolor on paper, 1874

George N. Cross

MEMORIES OF MY CHILDHOOD IN PLEASANT VALLEY

by

George N. Cross

forward by

Arthur Nicholson III
Tenney High School, Class of 1963
Methuen Educator/Administrator, 1968 to present

introduction and notes
by

J. Godsey

SICPRESS 2012
METHUEN, MASS

George Cross' *Memories of My Childhood* is an unpublished manuscript on deposit with the Lawrence Public Library's Special Collections.

Cover illustration: Homework: Winslow Homer (1836-1910), watercolor on paper, 1874. The Arkell Museum, Canajoharie, NY.

Thank you to the Cross family for the donation of a copy of the manuscript.

edited by J. Godsey
for copies sales@SicPress.com
Methuen, MA 2012

Table of Contents

Forward

George Cross' story is fascinating, especially for those of us who grew up in Methuen and the Merrimack Valley. It is a vivid picture and historical account of rural life in the 1800's of a small town in northeastern Massachusetts along the Merrimack River between two emerging and thriving cities, Lawrence and Haverhill. His detailed descriptions of Pleasant Valley itself, his old home and the ways of the household and farm, his school days, Civil War at home and Thanksgiving holidays are extraordinary. One gets a real flavor of a bygone era in our nation's development and history.

Spending summers as a youth on a Maine farm and having been a teacher and principal in Methuen for many years, I can relate deeply to what Cross penned in his memoir when he wrote that the daily tasks of the farm were drilled into his mind just as lastingly as rules of syntax. To be sure, the endnotes were most helpful in fully understanding the text of his writings.

George N. Cross was a true Renaissance man of his day. His Yankee values and pride in his community and family and who he was certainly comes through. I enthusiastically recommend this book, particularly to those interested in local history and the firsthand memories provided by the author.

Arthur Nicholson
Methuen, Mass.

Introduction

As I work on resurrecting many Merrimack Valley histories, I stumble upon stories I feel must be shared as soon as possible. George Cross' memoir of growing up in Methuen has been the most exciting new discovery thus far. He tells his story with such detail; one feels right at home in Methuen of 1860. The smells and the tastes evoke, not necessarily a simpler time but an honest and more honorable era, where one worked hard for even the food on your table and were grateful for the smallest of good fortunes. Fortunately, for the citizens of Methuen, Cross's grandson, Dr. Ernest Cross, Jr. donated a copy of this manuscript to local archives; sharing his grandfather's voice from the past, which is as fresh as if he had written this yesterday.

George Cross was born in Methuen, July 26, 1853, the son of Samuel and Lydia (Frye) Cross. Both his paternal and maternal ancestors were among the first settlers of Methuen, and his great, great, grandfather, Colonel James Frye, made a distinguished record in the Revolutionary war.

Cross was educated in the ungraded one room District Six school house in Pleasant Valley, within yards of his family's farmhouse. To attend the town high school he walked three miles every morning and afternoon for a year and half. When he could no longer attend he educated himself, rising to study before even the crows. With such an effort, George entered Philips Academy Andover and graduated ahead of his contemporaries, earning the Means Prize in Oration. He went on to graduate Phi Beta Kappa from Amherst College in 1876, and achieved Masters degrees. On a visit home in 1877, he met his future wife, Mary Sawyer of Atkinson, N. H., while she as school mistress of that District Six Pleasant Valley school house, boarded with the Cross family. They had two sons, Dr. Ernest S. Cross, an eminent physician and Harold N. Cross a successful engineer.

Beginning his life's work as an educator, Cross served as principal of Johnson High School at North Andover and taught at Ipswich High School, before arriving at the Robinson Female Seminary in 1883. It was a critical time in the history of the school, after thirteen years with its funds depleted, it was in decline. With gradual, and painstaking effort, in only a few years Cross raised the institution's profile from an obscure school possessing nothing but extensive grounds and a great bare, unfurnished building, to an institution of learning known all over New England.

Robinson Seminary became one of the most beautiful school buildings in the country; years before art decoration in schools became accepted, Cross had hung the walls of his school with costly and beautiful pictures and lined corridors with casts of Greek and Roman sculpture. Cross used every piece of artwork to further the lessons in history, mythology, or literature, as well as the history of art. Robinson Seminary was the second school in the country to introduce domestic science into its curriculum; its demonstration kitchen was used a model to be adopted by hundreds of schools, thus teaching his students the dignity of domesticity, self-dependence, and the ability to earn an honorable livelihood. Even a post-graduate course was offered to graduates who desired to teach, producing many of New England's most inspired teachers.

In 1905, after twenty-two years at the Robinson Seminary, still a young man, Cross retire to take up his twin passions oration and travel. As a writer and lecturer, he continued his work as an educator. He and his wife traveled the world and brought the excitement of art and history to new audiences on the lecture circuit. He became a very popular lecturer, speaking abroad as well as regularly at his alma maters. Cross was also a lecturer for the boards of education of New York City and Newark, N.J. until failing health force him to give up his work.

The Cross family were summer residents of Randolph, N. H. for nearly fifty years, and "Burnbrae," his home, was the first in what has become a large summer colony. He was a founder of the Randolph Mountain Club as in his younger days, he had tramped much over the mountain trails and he had a wide knowledge of the peaks and their legends. In 1924 he wrote, Randolph, Old and New, a history of that town, and in 1927 Dolly Copp and the pioneers of the Glen, a White Mountain related history. It is during this time that he penned his "Memories of My Childhood" about growing up in Pleasant Valley, Methuen, Mass, during the 1860s.

George Cross died December 30, 1930, at the age of 77, in Haverhill, Massachusetts, after a long illness. In the words of Dr. Ernest Cross, Jr.: "I remember him well, a man of 5' 11", stockily built with gray hair, and twinkling blue eyes, a boy at heart, delighted with the simplest of pleasures."

Besides his grandchildren and their descendants, with his memoir George Cross leaves a lasting legacy to the people of Methuen and the Merrimack Valley.

J. Godsey
Methuen, Mass.

I. Pleasant Valley

Pleasant Valley is not on the map. If you wish to find it, you will drive down the river road from the city of Lawrence on the western bank of the Merrimac toward Haverhill. Not quite half way between those prosperous cities, you will mark a place where three roads meet. Over the hill from the river straggles the abandoned Ferry[1] road to complete an old time "four corners.[2]" In the angle of the Ferry and Lawrence roads,[3] you will see a very ancient house. My old home.[4] is so camouflaged that even my fond eyes can scarcely recognize it. It swarms with a populace whose tongue I cannot understand.

But the old home is not more altered than the other features of Pleasant Valley. Where the little white school-house nestled among the great pine trees, a two story concrete[5] monstrosity looms in treeless barrenness. Across the orchard where I staked out his desert island and played Robinson Crusoe, the engineers are laying out city streets. Along the road where I drove the oxen in clouds of dust, the trolleys whiz and over its tarvia[6] surface motor cars glide. Tall houses, shops, and garages have clambered up across the "hill pasture" to the very top. Over the fields along the bank of the Merrimac, where Father[7] turned the long furrows and cradled and "stuked" his rye, the vast factories of the city of Lawrence loom.

The Pleasant Valley of my day was worthy of its name. It was both pleasant and beautiful. Nature had done much for it. The Ice Age made it and sculptured it and left as its western boundary a long drumlin-like ridge. The highest part of that ridge we knew as "Webster's Hill"[8] on whose summit stood four enormous pine trees, landmarks for miles around. From Webster's Hill the wooded range trended northward for a couple of miles, then turned eastward to close the valley on the north. The eastern boundary beyond the low hill, on whose slope lay our farm, was the beautiful Merrimac. The broad, noble river sweeping northward, midway of the valley divided its waters to flow around a low green island. Beyond, the united waters broke through the hills in a narrow gorge and went rushing down the boulder-strewn channel of Mitchell's falls[9]with a road that, in time of flood, could be heard a mile away. The valley abounded in beautiful brooks that fed the great river. One little stream was to me a companion and playfellow. It came out of the alders near the top of a hill, flowed alongside out garden, and went on its way through a long covered culvert under the road. It was a dancing, singing, merry little brook willing, when I harnessed it with a dam of turf and stones, to turn my water wheels night and day.

From Webster's Hill you looked down upon a checkered landscape of plowed fields, orchards, pastures, and belts of woods. The alluvial soil of the level lands along the river was very fertile with never a stone to plague the ploughshare. The orchards in spring were always white with fragrant bloom and, in autumn, yielded hundreds of barrels of fine apples.

In the morning, the sun came bustling up from behind our hill, with a businesslike air and little color. But at night as we sat on the warm front door step, he sank down in the stately majesty beyond Webster's Hill and spread across the west a curtain of scarlet and purple and gold.

There was no poverty in Pleasant Valley and no wealth, only degrees of prosperity. We had neighborhood quarrels but no feuds: jealousies were soon forgiven and forgotten. My own memories, together with a clear recollection of Father's reminiscences of his own boyhood picturesquely told by the fireside on winter evenings, enable me to write of a rural New England life almost a century ago–of ways, customs, and faiths, so different from those of today, it will not seem that such things could have been only sixty years ago. But sixty years back is a long period now, we live so much in a single year. Today we unfold our newspapers, damp from the press, morning and evening and, in times of excitement, buy an extra at noon. Sixty years ago, I saw the official town crier[10], in tall silk hat and long linen duster, going his rounds in Lawrence. At the street corners, he stopped, rang his bell, and, as the passersby paused to listen, read in a drawling monotone: week-old local happenings, much older foreign events, auctions to be, bargains in house, lots to be had.

There lies before me, an old account book in which Father made occasional entries of transactions charged to neighbors from 1838 to 1870. In the winter, nearly all the menfolk made slippers and shoes[11]. Father kept a horse and small wagon which the neighbors hired to carry their finished "sets" of shoes to the village or to Haverhill and bring back new stocks of leather. The charge for the trip to the village, three miles distant and requiring a half day or more, was uniformly twenty-five cents[12]. Milk was delivered for two or three cents a cord. A tenement was rented for a dollar per month[13]

The coming of the Civil War and war prices in 1861 and the rapid growth of Lawrence and Haverhill which opened nearby markets for all farm produce brought new ways of life, and great prosperity to Pleasant Valley.

II. The Old Home

BE IT E'RE SO HUMBLE
THERE'S NO PLACE LIKE HOME

· The old house stood close by the road, a large square to-story structure built by the carpenter from whom Father bought it when a very young man. The front and ends were painted white, the back red, an economy widely practiced in old New England because red ochre cost far less than white lead. In from of the house grew a noble elm, the tallest tree of its kind I ever saw, towering far above the top of the chimney. Baltimore Orioles swung their cradles from the drooping branches and reared their young, all day long filling the tree-top with song. Between the tree and the house was Mother's flower garden. Mother[1] loved flower and found ways to have them. With gentle tact, she enlisted us all in their cultivation. Even Father toiled many hours in the flower garden thinking regretfully of the weeds among the potatoes. So, all summer about the house were bright bloom and pleasant odors.

A broad path bordered with pinks led up through the garden to the front door. Narrower ones on each side led away to beds of double buttercups, ladies delight, and pink yarrow. Beyond blossomed wygelia, peonies, bleeding heart, drove in the nest and poor man's shillings. Between the front windows of the living room, grew giant mock orange, whose far descendant, now stands beside the porch of my summer home, and each June, its perfume wafts me back and under the window of Mother's garden. By the south window flourished a snow drop, and under the window of Mother's room grew a yellow rose bush. Of that wonderful yellow rose bush, more shall be said later. Over the south door, climbed a Queen Prairie Rose, which in its season formed a triumphal arch of pink loveliness above that entrance. Until I saw the gardens of England, I had never seen such roses as bloomed at the south end of the house for love of Mother. In the midst of the garden were two cherry trees, that in May were banks of white bloom and in July handed out great clusters of blood red Oxhearts to us and the birds alike, enough for all.

Behind the house, was the vegetable garden where, in neat beds, we raised all sorts of good things for the autumn and winter table. In the border next to the house the big red buds of the rhubarb, we called it "Pie Weed[2]", pushed up very early. Down in the corner by the "rollway[3]" was a tangled group of lilacs, that each year hung out their fragrant thyrsi.[4] A vine on the wall by the Ferry road gave us fine white grapes. In the angle of the pasture wall was a flat-topped boulder, on which we dressed the shad. At the foot of the garden beyond the rows of currant and gooseberry bushes, was a stone curbed spring into whose cool depths night and morning we lowered the cans of milk, to go a few hours later to the city to feed the babies. By the corner of the house stood the well house sheltering the windlass, over which wound the long rope that drew up dripping buckets of delicious water. Between the well house and the piggery, we used to set the barrel coops in which the mother hens kept house for the black and yellow chicks running in and out among the growing vegetables. Beyond the well house was the clothes yard where every Monday morning waved the family wash, a half hour ahead of any of the neighbors. A path led over easy, flat stepping stones in the wall to the pasture lane here, in the late afternoon, the cows waited for me to lower the bars and let them into the barn for the milking.

It is pleasant to linger out here in the sunshine among birds and flowers and growing things but I ought to ask you into the house, for your visit, by the little-used front door. By the sidelight hung the ancient thermometer to tell us when to shiver and when to resume our cotton shirts. The front door opened into a very small entry nearly filled by narrow crooked stairs leading up to two large front rooms above. Into the living rooms at the right, you shall be invited later, there to spend an evening and get acquainted with the whole family. At the left is the parlor, the room of formal state and utter desolation. It is seldom opened except for weddings, funerals, the pastoral calls of the minister and similar solemnities. On the floor is the one carpet in the house; on the center table rests the big ornate family Bible. In the corner, stands a "whatnot"[5] on which are arranged seashells, a few specimens of minerals and curios of various kinds. A row of daguerreotypes stands across the mantel above which hands a hair wreath,[6] into whose flowers my sister[7] has conscientiously wrought a lock of hair of every family connection unto the third and fourth generation. On the walls hang several pictures in "coral" frames. The "coral frames" are of home manufacturer. We first made a frame of pinewood which we covered with a coat of soft putty. Then we dyed grains of rice in melted red sealing wax and stuck them artistically all over the putty which presently dried hard. The "coral frames" were pretty and effective for several years until the hungry mice got into the parlor and nibbled off the rice.

The huge chimney at the center around which the rooms were built occupied almost half the house. We had four great cavernous, hospitable fireplaces. But we were too economical to enjoy any of them for the era of the "airtight" stove had just dawned. The fireplaces were closed with iron fire boards before which were set up cook stoves of those sheet iron abominations.

The rooms on the back, or east side of the house, were more interesting. In the south-east corner was a sleeping room known as "Mother's room." Thither I went with Mother for interviews of private nature. I was not a bad boy but Mother was a stern disciplinarian. She believed "spare the rod and spoil the child". She did her duty as she saw it. And that is why I am so good now.

At the north end of the house behind the back stairs was the cool "buttry" where the milk was "set" and the butter churned. The kitchen was a long, low, dark room lighted by two small east windows, the floor painted yellow, the walls, a depressing lead color.

But life and work and bustle made the kitchen always a cheery place. The big fire-place and the bigger brick oven filled all the side opposite the windows. A door in the corner let you plunge suddenly down a steep, terrible flight of steps unto the blackness of the cellar. The door led up the crooked back stairs to an immense unfinished room where many of the household tasks were performed. Here the family spinning used to be done. But Grandmother had finished her life work, and her wheel had been consigned to the attic before I could remember.

From the "back chamber" a door with a hole in it for the convenience of the cat in her mousing opened up on the attic stairs. The attic was at once attic, granary, and cold storage rooms. Under the south windows were hung bins always full of oats, rye and barley. We never grew wheat. From hooks in the rafters hung spareribs, chines[8] of pork, links of sausages, a quarter of beef frozen solid for winter keeping. Drying on the floor were a hundred or more bushels of ears of corn. If you wished to know just how many bushels we raised any year, you consulted, under that date, the tally chalked up on the rafters above your head. There, along the rafters, were the records of the lean years and the fat years, the prosperity and the adversity of the old farm.

This was the home of my boyhood, a hive of industry with few idle, and fewer unhappy days.

III. The Ways of the Household

*She looketh well to the ways of the household a
nd eateth not the bread of idleness.*

The kitchen was the center of our household activities, as the living room was of our social life. There were performed a great variety of tasks many of which modern inventions have rendered obsolete. In the early winter, we dipped or ran the year's supply of candles. On the bricks in front of the stove, we placed two brass kettles, one empty, one filled with molten tallow. On small sticks, we suspended lengths of candle wicking about two inches apart. These we dipped in the tallow and hung across the empty kettle to drip and cool. This process of dipping and cooling was repeated till something of a candle was formed round each wick. The ill shaped drips were then made more symmetrical and finished by cautiously pouring dipperfuls of tallow down over them. Later we had candle molds that would run a dozen candles each. Into each tube of the mold, we dropped the wicking, knotted it, and drew it back tight to close the small end of the tube and keep the wick in the center. It was an easy matter then to fill the mold with tallow, set it away to cool and the next morning, cut the knots in the wicks and draw forth twelve shapely shining candles. It took a long time to dip or run enough candles for, until the invention of better illuminants; we used hundreds of candles every year.

In winter, we churned in the kitchen. When my arms had grown strong enough, I became the motive power for the churn. It was a task I rather liked for I could turn the crank with one hand and the pages of an interesting book with the other. It was sometimes a long task it grew harder and harder through the thickening cream. When patience and the book were almost at an end there would come a sudden change. Something was giving way and the turning was very easy: I could hear the buttermilk splashing and the clots of butter dropping from the paddles; a few more turns and I would announce, "The butter has come." Then my task was ended but there were further steps interesting to watch. The buttermilk was drawn off at the bottom of the churn and a pail of cold water added. The crank revolved a few times with a loud splashing and Mother lifted out the great golden nugget and laid it on the butter board. How she patted and rolled and squeezed it in her large white hands, working out the buttermilk. Then the salt was added and more patting and rolling and squeezing. In her left hand she took the wooden stamp; with her right she broke off from the nugget a half pound, never a bit more nor a bit less, pressed it down on the stamp rounding and smoothing the pat and dexterously slipping it off onto the waiting platter. There was the golden "print" edged with a circle of stars, a blossoming four-leafed clover at the center. And the luck of the clover was always in Mother's golden butter.

I have not so distinct a memory of the cheese making for that was given up when I was very young. I recall the adding of the rennet to the hot milk, the squeezing of the curds in the cheese press and the when running along the channels into a pan on the floor. I remember the long row of green cheeses on a shelf in the "back chamber." Mother's basting each cheese with butter and leaving them to ripen in the sun.

Saturday was baking day. We were early risers and ate breakfast in the kitchen by candle light, except on the longest summer days. After breakfast, while the "rye and injun" were being sifted out for brown bread[1] and the Indian pudding[2], the menfolk brought in armfuls of "oven wood" and built a fire in the brick oven. When the oven fire had burned down, the coals were shoveled into the stove and the brick floor swept clean with the oven broom. The brick oven was a huge, domed cavern so large that I often crawled into it and circled round in it wondering if Rob Roy would not have liked such a hiding place[3]. When the oven was in readiness, the pots of beans[4], the crocks of brown bread, Indian pudding, and pan dowdy[5], were placed on the flat oven shovel and pushed far into the cavern. The mouth was closed with a wooden cover and the contents left to simmer and bake slowly in the mellow heat all night. I have no words with which to do justice to the Sunday morning breakfast which the long wooden hook that for a hundred years, had hung by the oven mouth drew out from our old brick oven. One of the pleasant memories to my wife and myself, of a sojourn in Florence at the famous Villa Trollope[6], is or our landlady a New England woman, setting before us on a Saturday night a steaming plate of beans and brown bread, the beans baked in a pot imported from Boston.

On Saturday, Mother always fried a great pan-full of doughnuts[7]. It had to be a large pan to last over Sunday. Once when we were enjoying at dinner a plate of Mother's doughnuts, grave Uncle Hiram[8] amazed us all with this scintillation, "George, when you have eaten the doughnut what becomes of the HOLE?" quick witted Mother instantly replied, "My Uncle Hiram, if the doughnut is as good as one of mine you will eat the WHOLE!" But the retort was too abstruse for Uncle Hiram.

The making of Mother's fried cranberry turnovers[9]. Cranberry turnovers recipe is a lost art. And the world is poorer for it. She used to roll out the pastry as for the doughnuts; with a plate, she cut out circles of the pastry, filled the centers with cranberry sauce; folded over the edges and in some mysterious way fastened them together securely enough to resist the expansion of the sauce in frying. No modern cook can do that. The attempt results in a frying kettle filled with boiling fat and cranberry sauce and a despairing cook.

The discovery of a plateful of those brown juicy beauties on the buttery shelf was an occasional for strategy and this dialogue would ensue; I (in the buttery), "Mother may I have a turnover?" (Mother in the kitchen), "No, George, there are just enough for dinner." I (in the buttery), "But Mother, I have bitten on." Mother, "Well then I suppose you will have to eat it." And I did!

Coffee roasted and ground was unknown in our day. We could buy only the dried berry. The Saturday task, after the kitchen floor had been washed and everything made tidy, was to put on the spider and roast the coffee. It was work of delicate art for Mother seated by the stove with a long charred wooden paddle in one hand and *Godey's Lady's Book*[10] in the other. She stirred and stirred, the rolling kernels grew brown, and the mass never took fire in spite of the attractions of Godey. The kitchen became thick with smoke and the pleasant aroma of the roasting pervaded the house.

It was in the kitchen in the autumn we pared and strung apples for many evenings. We liked to do two bushels an evening and sometimes our ambition soared to a barrel. I presided at the apple parer screwed to the table with a bushel basketful of apples at my left hand and a pan for the pared ones at the right. My sister cored and quartered them; Father, with a darning needle threaded with shoe thread, strung the quarters in long festoons for the drying racks. Mother was our entertainer and exempted from all duty of the apples. In her clear, tireless voice sounding above the clatter of my parer evening after evening, she read to us *Gibbon's Decline and Fall*[11]. Sometimes now, as we motor about in the remoter rural New England, we see a few festoons of apples hanging against the house. To the rest of the family, I suppose, they are apples drying in the sun. But to me they are dates, battles, periods, epochs in Roman History strung on the thread of memory.

In the kitchen we made ready for the annual butchering, a necessary but, to me, terrible rite. Very early in the morning of the dread day the fire board before the fireplace and removed and three huge brass kettles of water for the scalding hung on the long crane over the fire. I always had to see and hear all the horrors of the butchering for I was the official deputed to bring, at the command of the executioner, the sharpened knife with which to do the deed.

It is the boast of Squires Packing House[12] that it utilizes everything of the porker but the squeal. We allowed the squeal to escape regretfully and because we know, we could hear plenty more from the little squealers growing up in the pen. We found ways to use every scrap of our slaughtered animals except the liver. When we cut up a hog, we never forgot to hang, on a nail in the wagon house, a piece of otherwise unused pork with which to grease the saws at the woodpile in winter. A little bundle of the whitest and stiffest bristles was always tied up and put away in the box of cobblers tools to be twisted into the "waxed ends" for sewing needles.

On a shelf in the cellar way, stood three earthen crocks in which was saved every shred of animal fat not fit for food. The content of one crock was used for grease for the wooden axles of the farm wagon and ox cart. When Uncle Hiram's "rhuematiz" warned us of the coming of a "spell of wet," we set the second crock down before the fire, stirred lampblack into the melting fat, and coated our boots generously. The dressing was a "two in one," waterproofing and shoe polish. I well remember the first shoe brush and box of blacking my brother brought home and the sarcasm Father leveled at him. "Dude," he would have called him had that word been coined.

The third crock received the "soap grease." At intervals, the soap wagon of L. Beach and Son[11] called at our door. The blue-frocked driver took all our "soap grease," weighed out all our ashes, of which we had many bushels, and loaded into his wagon every bone I had gathered. The bones were my perquisite and paid for in cash, which I thriftily deposited down the chimney of my red tin bank. The other things were bartered for bars of yellow soap and that synonym of flattery "soft soap."

"The nearer the bone, the sweeter the meat." If this little review of our Spartan economies, our cheerful sacrifices made without a thought that they were sacrifices may encourage some one who is struggling today to make the ends meet. I shall be well rewarded,

IV. Ways of the Farm

On the western shore of the Merrimac below, Mitchells Falls in the city of Haverhill lay two old millstones. They were placed there by the Hannah Dustin[1] landed from her perilous canoe voyage down the Merrimac after tomahawking a dozen of her Indian captors. Those ancient millstones have ground many grists from our farm.

A trip to Bradley's Mill[2] was always an important even in my boyhood. It began in the attic, filling sacks with ears of corn and carrying them down the cooked stairs to be loaded on the big wagon. Three miles down the river road toward Haverhill, we turned into a narrow lane winding between ferny, flowery bank on one side and on the other a little foaming stream just escaped from its job at the mill and hurrying down to the river. Bradley's Grist Mill stood in a very picturesque spot. It was a narrow, weather blackened, two story building standing besides the dam over which flowed a white sheet of water from the placid mill pond behind. From the ferny bank at the foot of a huge overspreading willow, a rickety covered gallery crossed to the second story of the mill. We used to stop under the willow, carry out sacks of corn along the gallery, and empty them into the hopper in the second story. Then we drove along the lane down round a sharp curve under the gallery to the mill door in the first story. On the first floor, we found the meal pouring in a warm golden stream from between the whirling millstones. The miller, Lo Bradley, in his long frock and wonderful meal-covered hat was always hurrying about, up and down the stairs and through the noisy, cob-webbed rooms. Miller Bradley had a terrible impediment of speech. When he attempted to speak, he threw his head far back, opened his mouth very wide, gasped and sputtered till you were thoroughly alarmed, and at last fired out the words in a high squeaky voice. But his remarks, when safely delivered, were shrewd and witty. Father and the miller were always in a road of laughter from the pouring of the first sacks of corn into the hopper till the toll had been measured from the meal and the last sack loaded on the wagon at the lower door.

The faithful care of the animals on the farm brought, beside the profits of the flocks, companionship and a mutual affection that is pleasing. The first robin's song in the spring was not more gratifying than the joy of the cows when on the twentieth of May, always the twentieth of May, we swung open the barnyard gate to let them go down to the lower pasture. How they kicked up their heels, waved tails in the air, playfully hooked each other, priced and cavorted in elephantine gambols, bellowing, "Spring has come and we are glad!"

The modern dairyman has a theory that southing surroundings for the cows at milking time, a tempting fodder, (even cheerful music has been suggested) are conducive to a better flow of milk. I put that theory in practice years and years ago, repeating in a pleasant tone to the cows as I milked them pages of Latin grammar, the conjugation of irregular Greek verbs with what effect upon the flow of milk I shall never know.

"Pony" was the horse of all work. She was a blooded Morgan mare from Vermont, a shapely spirited animal with a very glossy chestnut coat. She was a willing worker and a good roadster. But Pony had a bad disposition. She desired to kick to death or devour every person but Father who approached her. With Father, she was gentle, even affectionate and he worshipped her. As a small boy, Pony terrorized me kicking and leering at me with wide-open mouth every time I entered the stable. The time came when I could stand it no longer. One day in Father's absence, I applied the handle of a hoe to Pony's sleek flanks till we arrived at a mutual understanding. After that, Pony was as obsequious to me as to Father. But I never liked her, never harnessed her for errands. Pony abode on the farm drawing great loads, kicking and biting for almost forty years.

We took pleasure and pride in our big oxen. "Swapping" oxen was Father's chief diversion and excitement. I have now the long fine linked steel chain with which he "girted[3]" the oxen. No matter what were the markings of the new pair, the near ox was once christened "Star" and the off one, "Bright." He would wave the goad stick over them like a wand, lay it gently across their horns, touch Bright with it and say cheerily, "Gee up Bright," pat Star's neck and shout, "Now get up." And they always "got up." I learned to drive the oxen in the same kindly way, used them much, and came to have a real liking for the patient slow moving giants.

Some years after I left the farm, on Saturday afternoon, I was on my way to make a social call clad in tall silk hat and long frock coat, the proper habiliments of a young high school principal. As I reached the centre of the village, I saw a pair of oxen coming down the hill drawing a sled load of green wood. As they came into the village square, they ran upon a spot of bare ground and stuck fast. The driver, as green as the wood, from his perch on the load lashed with a long whip and clucked, trying to drive the oxen like a pair of horses. Even the most patient oxen will resent such an insult. Making my way through the grinning crowd around the sled, I took the whip from the astonished fellow's hand, knotted the lash to the stock, and waved my improvised goad stick over the oxen. I laid it gently across their horns, touched "Bright" with it, and patted "Star's" neck. Then I shouted,

"Now get up" and they "got up." They threw their great shoulders against the walnut bows, humped their backs, and dragged that scraping, grinding load across to "good sledding." Then I place myself at the heads of my oxen, shouldered the goad stick, cocked my tall hat parallel and marched triumphantly down the street with my team and turned into the yard where the wood was to be delivered. I made my call a little diffidently conscious that my silk hat was stick all over with cattle hairs and that I must smell "as strong as an ox."

Corn grew, grain ripened, potatoes gave their increase, sixty years ago just as they do now. But our methods of cultivating and harvesting them were very different. But we had never heard of sowing grain in drills, of planting potatoes between the layers of damp straw, of spraying fruit trees. We never had a McCormick Universal Harvester, but our mode of harvesting rye in its small way was thrifty. I have not seen a cradle for fifty years. It consisted of a scythe with an attachment of long, wooden fingers parallel to it. As the mower swung his cradle through the standing grain, the straws were caught on the fingers. By a dexterous backward movement of the cradle, the grain was laid in an even, orderly swath, not a straw escaping. Ruth would never have gleaned behind the reapers in our field.[4] The grain was then tied into sheaves for stacking or carried directly to the barn.

On the clean swept threshing (we called it "thrashing") floor we laid down two rows of sheaves six in a row with the heads inward. It required strong arms and some skill to sing a flail all day. A wrong swing of a stroke out of time meant a bruised elbow or head. There is music in the rhythmic beat-beat of the two flails on the heads of grain while the flying, bounding kernels of rye beat a tattoo on the floor. Twice we thrashed and turned the sheaves. The empty, clean straw, tied up again into bundles sold for more than the best timothy.

We swept the grain into a heap at one side of the threshing floor for the winnowing. We brought in the big red fanning mill and placed it in the middle of the barn floor. Father officiated at the crank while I shoveled the grain into the hopper of the roaring, clanking mill. A blast of chaff roared clear back to the barn door. The grains of rye dropped downward from sieve to sieve and flowed a bright stream into the measure of the floor.

We knew no Volsted Law[5], made much cider, and sold much vinegar. No one ever went from our door the worse for our hospitality. In the autumn, we moved about the dooryard through lanes of waiting cider barrels. Father's adze drumming on the empty casks as he repaired them, made pleasant music. When our week came to use the cider mill,[6] there were stirring times. The oxen backed loads of cider apples to the door of the mill. At the centre of the mill stood the "grinde." Above a vat rose a stout frame supporting a gear of three deeply corrugated, upright wooden cylinders, the "nuts" of the grinder. From the central nut of the gear, a stout beam curved nearly to the ground to which we hitched Pony to travel round and round the vat and turn the grinder. Father carried shovelfuls of apples from that cart to the hopper of the mill, timing his trips to Pony's return along her orbit. My duty was to "scrape the nuts." Seated on a board across the vat under the creaking beam with a paddle in each hand, I scraped down the corrugations of the nuts as they became packed full of the dripping apple pulp. It was a "soft job" yet conducive of backache.

Near the grinder stood the press on which we spread the apple pulp with alternate layers of clean rye straw. Two stout men at the ends of the ends of the long capstan bars could apply a tremendous squeeze to the press. What fun it was to watch the first drops appearing, then the little streams running down the "pumice," then the little brooks of frothing brown sweetness flowing down into the hogshead[7].

Sometimes now I seat myself at a soda fountain, thrust the artificial straw into my foaming glass and try to think I am imbibing sweet cider at the bung hole of a barrel in the dark old mill, the smell of apples everywhere, Pony going round and round, and the juice dripping down the press. But it is all a poor substitute.

V. A Winter Evening in the Living Room

I must not depict the life of the boy on the farm sixty years ago as all work and no play, for we had lots of fun. There were skating, coasting, fishing, and the school games of which I have written elsewhere. But in the home where there was no Victrola, no piano, cards and dancing forbidden, few books, one thin magazine, one weekly paper, what were out recreations and amusements? For answer, I will relate nothing that was not at some time an actual occurrence. But you will grant me, in these prosy pages, the poetic license of bringing into the hours of a short winter's evening memories of scenes and events enjoyed over a period of years.

The living room is a large square room in the southwest corner of the house. A huge cook stove stands before what should have been a blazing fireplace; a china closet fills one corner opposite and a secretary with green baize doors the other. On the west side of the room under the clock, is a table with a turkey red covering on which stands a big dish of apples, another of fruits and a corn popper. In the corner, by the stove, is a huge wood box piled high with dry wood. In the center of the room is a tall light stand on which burn four or five candles in shining brass and iron candlesticks. The floor is almost covered with braided and drawn in rugs.

By the secretary in the corner, my brother[1] and the schoolmaster are playing "fox and geese[2]" with kernels of corn for the geese and a pumpkin seed for the fox. On one side of the light stand, Mother is knitting, on the other side Sister, with a great basket of "holy" socks in her lap, is doing the family darning and Uncle Hiram sits by the wood box to replenish the fire, for he is the family stoker. Between Uncle Hiram and the door, sit two of Father's woodchoppers. They are eccentric fellows, but very likable upon acquaintance.

Father is seated in his rocking chair by the stove, reading the *Boston Courier*. The cat, who objects to the drafty floor, is settled on his knee. She sometimes expresses her joy at the warmth of her perch by clawing into his trousers, calling forth wrathful protests from the reader. It is a pleasant peaceful picture, Father slowly rocking, an old black hat on the back of his head, his silver bowed spectacles on his nose, the paper outstretched, a lighted candle held very close to the printed page in his left hand. No wonder that presently his head nods and presently occurs what I have been anticipating with unholy joy—the newspaper caches fire. Jennie springs to take the candle from his nerveless hand, the cat makes a wild leap to the floor, and Mother stuffs the burning paper into the stove.

The catastrophe has fully awakened Father, and he is ready to talk and recall reminiscences of his boyhood; how he used to whittle out shoe pegs[3] and sell them at the village for a cent a hundred; how his mother used to make bean porridge in an iron pot, put a rope end into the pot and let it freeze; how he used to drive the oxen into the woods with a mold of the frozen porridge tied to every sled stake and the iron pot slung over his arm.

Telling about how he went shad fishing, he said, "When the Shadbush grew white in the spring woods, we used to caulk the boat, overhaul the seine[4] and row up the river to a long beach of white sand at a place called the 'Gerrymander', in memory of Elbridge Gerry and his political schemes.[5] And, there we would fish for several days if the shad ran well. We lived in a shanty on at the beach. We generally got the best hauls early in the morning. We would load the seine in the stern of the boat and two men would row up to a maple on the bank and I would walk up on the shore. Then I would pick up a long rope hitched to the end of the seine. One man in the boat would row straight out more than half way across the river, the man in the stern paying out the seine. The net had cork floats on one edge and lead sinkers on the other so it would stand upright in the water. When the net was all paid out, the boatman rowed slowly down the river. I kept even with it, walking down the shore, and holding tight my rope. Opposite the shanty, the boat was headed in toward our shore. Then came the excitement. Inside the curve of bobbing floats the water would be all bubbly, heads would appear and tails fluke. When we had drawn the net clear ashore, there flopping and gasping on the sand would be all sorts of fish – chubs and suckers and pumpkinseeds and perch and sometimes as many as fifty silvery shad."

"One morning a big sturgeon was swimming up the river and ran his nose right into our net. He pushed and we pulled and we thought we were going to land the big shark. But just before we got him to shoal water, he broke through the net and went scooting up the river toward Lawrence. We spent all the rest of that day mending our net. "

"What did you do with the shad," I asked.

"We parceled them out among the crew and the neighbors. Sometimes I hitched up the horse, put a shoe box full of fish in the hind end of the wagon and peddled them out and made sometimes quite a spec."

He would go on, "One summer I examined the crows in arithmetic. I found that they could count two but couldn't get up quite so high as three,"

"How did you do that Father?" I asked.

"That spring we planted the acre piece below the barn to corn. When it came up the crows went to pulling it like a fury. I would creep down past the barn with the gun. But before I was within gun shot, they would be off and one old fellow would light on the top of the dead elm on the river bank and caw and holler and laugh till I got mad. I cut some bushes and built a little booth around the butt of the sweet tree at the edge of the corn. And there I would hide with my gun. But never a crow would come nigh and then, when I got tired and went home, the critters would come hollering and settle on the corn. One morning I took Nelson, with a big stick over his shoulder, into the booth. After a while, I sent him back to the house with his stick at shoulder arms. But it didn't work. I could hear the old watchman crow hollering, 'look out, only one of 'em has come out. The other feller is in there.' The next day, I took Nelson and Jerome down with me and sent them both back together with their sticks over their shoulders. Then the whole cawing caboodle came and settled down on the corn. In less than half an hour, I was hanging up two dead crows among the corn as a warning to them to study their arithmetic more. But I have gabbed enough, Come, Leander, let's have one of your stories."

And the all French Canadian woodchopper tilts forward his chair, consigns to the fire his chaw of gum (tobacco is taboo in Mother's domain), scratched his curly head and begins. Would that I could, transfer his picturesque patois to these pages.

"When I was a young man, I lived in the valley of the noble St. Lawrence down below Quebec. I knew well all the people of who I shall speak tonight. And the story I shall relate is true. There lived on two fine adjoining farms near my home the families of Jean leBlanc and Basil St. Roque. Monsieur and Madame LeBlanc had four fine stalwart sons and the St. Roques as many beautiful daughters. It was the dream of the parents that love and then marriage might ensue between the young people and that would unite the two noble farms. Then they would be spared the division into many narrow strips running back from the river, non wide enough for the land of the cows. I think the beautiful daughters were not averse to matrimony. But no progress could be made toward that end because of that very excruciating bashfulness of the young men. Why, if one of the LeBlanc boys were in the field hoeing the corn and caught sight of the fluttering skirts of a pretty St. Roque maiden approaching, the poor lad would drop his hoe and run to the woods."

"One day as the St. Roques were sitting down to dinner in the kitchen, there came a timid knock at the door. One of the lovely daughters hastened to open the door. Oh, joy! Without stood the eldest and finest and also the most bashful of the four LeBlanc sons. 'How do you do, John? Welcome! Come right in.' John, much excited, his face dripping with sweat, his eyes very large, cries, 'No, No! I cannot stop. I came over to–,' 'No matter what you came for now, John. You will come in and have the dinner with us,' and the hopeful father drags the silenced but resisting boy straight to the kitchen and places him down into the seat between the two loveliest daughters. Madam, the mother, is very smiling; the young ladies are as entertaining as they can be. The father loads John's plate. But it is all to no purpose. John cannot eat one mouthful nor speak one word. The sweat, it pours and pours. After a long time, John leaps to his feet and finds his tongue. I cannot stay another minute. I should not have stayed as long as I have. BECAUSE OUR HOUSE IS A FIRE AND I CAME OVER TO BORROW A LADDER."

Leander tilts his chair back, takes out another chew of gum, and is silent.

Sister looks up in surprise and says, "Is that the end?"

"Yes, Miss Jennie, do you not like my story?"

"Yes, but it ends too abruptly."

"How would you like it to end?"

"I would have had the four pretty girls help John rush the ladder over and do many brave things to save the house. I would have the girl's find courage put the boys to shame and admiration should spur them all to propose on the spot. In wedded bliss on the united farms they should live happily ever after."

"Yes, Miss Jennie, very pretty; but so it was not."

"Now, Billy," says Father, "Lets wind up the evening with some music."

While Billy, the other woodchopper, is gone upstairs after his violin, let me give a bit of his biography. Billy Richards would today be called a "blue jay," a "weary Willie[6]

"His comings and his goings were always unannounced. He was tall, thin to emaciation, hesitating and slouching in his gait. Billy could discern a pitcher of cider a far way off. He had never learned to read or write. But, he had opinions burning for expression on every subject. His one earthly possession was a beautiful old violin on whose worn stem we could decipher the word, Cremona[7]. He new not a note of written music, but any selection once heard was his never to be forgotten, possession to be beautifully reproduced on the Cremona. When he played he seated himself in a chair, threw his right leg over the left, beating time with his left foot on the floor, his thin body swaying, his eyes closed, his leathery, pockmarked, old face alight with the joy of it.

Billy had a habit silently resented by Mother of going about the house in warm weather barefooted. One evening he was entertaining us in that shoeless condition, when my wicked brother discovered a somnolent wasp on the windowsill. It was the work of a moment to transfer the wasp to a sheet of paper and slip it under Billy's bare, vibrating left foot. Results were obtained at once. The music ceased. Billy leaped from his fair with a wild yell and went hoping about the room on one foot making remarks not fit to print.

But Billy has returned with his violin and seated himself in his chair with bow poised. He knows Father's taste. First comes "Money Musk," then "Martilla's Lesson," "Old Dan Tucker," "Pop Goes The Weasel," "Yankee Doodle." Then the flying bow sobers down to "Annie Laurie", "the Old Oaken Bucket", and when the violin sings as only Billy can make it. "Shall Auld Acquaintance Be Forgotten," we all feelingly respond with the beautiful words.

At nine o'clock, Father takes a candle and goes to the kitchen to wind the tall clock. The squeaky screechy whine of the winding wheels sounding through the house is our curfew and we prepare for bed. Father takes a soft pine stick from behind the wood box and with his jack knife whittles shavings for the morning fire. Mother takes down from its shelf in the south window one of her pet geranium and tenderly carries it down cellar and leaves it in the arch under the chimney, the only spot in the house that will not be down to zero before morning while the thermometer outside the front door will mark thirty degrees below. All the animals at the barn have been made as comfortable as possible on this bitter night and Father has carried into the sty three bundles of corn stalks as extra bedclothes for the pigs. Hot bricks and flatirons are taken from the oven and wrapped in newspapers and strips of old flannel, solaces for the womenfolks. But we of sterner stuff scorn such effeminacies.

The candles are taken in hand, good night is said, and we go out several ways. The full moon shining in at the eastern windows saves the extravagance of a candle to light me to bed. The disrobing in a patch of moon light in my chamber is done with lightening speed. I never neglect the prayer

Sister taught me. But I shall have to say it in bed tonight. I leap into the arms of the deep feather bed and pull the foot thick stratum of comforters up around me. Grandmother's linen sheets are sheets of ice for a minute. Then I sink back on the pillow and listen.

How tense and keyed up everything is on such a night. It is the profound sleep of all Nature. Yet there are sounds creeping throughout the windless calm, clarion of roosters sleeping in the barn and dreaming it is morning, a cow thrashing her horns against her stanchion, a rat rolling an ear of corn around on the attic floor. I hear the distant booming and groaning of the pent up air under the ice in the current of the rushing river, the cracking and snapping of the frozen ground, the low crunching sound running along the snow. A hand wrought nail driven deep into a big timber contracting more and more in the intense cold, gives way with a report like a gun rousing the whole household to momentary consciousness. Then drowsiness steals over me and the sound sleep of healthy happy boyhood.

VI. In School Days

Still sits the school house by the road,
A ragged beggar running.
Around it still the sumacs grow,
And blackberry vines are running.[1]

In the midst of Pleasant Valley was located District School Number Six, the centre of all our interests. In other respects, the typical little red schoolhouse of New England ours was painted white. Many times, I pictured it on my slate, a pencil line of smoke always curling from the low chimney like a pig's tail. In front, two outer doors opened into the boys' and girl's entries. Inner doors always with two or three panels knocked out for ventilation and observation admitted of the school room.

The two entries built into the corners left a deep recess of alcove at the front of the schoolroom with a single window opening to the south and front end of the building. Here stood the teacher's desk, ponderous piece of furniture with a sloping front that lifted to disclose a deep cupboard for the school register, the teacher's books, the big hand bell, perhaps a ferule[2] or rawhide, the *Webster's Unabridged,* and a pile of copybooks more or less neatly arranged. The desk lid when raised afforded a screen behind which a harassed teacher might laugh or weep for a moment in relief of pent up emotions.

The carpenter who built that desk evidently took thought for the schoolmaster with very large feet for he build the enclosed space under it cavernous. But he built better than he knew for that cavern under the desk came to be a valued place for teaching humility and penitence. Many an impenitent urchin spent hours of quiet enjoyment there, depicting his cell walls with pencil or knife or bit of charcoal, his esteem for his jailer.

Under the window extended a seat the width of the alcove. On one end of the seat, stood the terrestrial globe, always an object of wonder to me. Above the other end of the seat, was space for another culprit. But it was never wise to dispose two rascals in the alcove seat and in the cavern at once, to grin and giggle in the shelter of the big desk.

The school-room itself was about eighteen by thirty feet, with three windows on each side and two in the rear. There were six rows of rude benches across the room, grading in height, from the leg length of very little chaps, up the needs of six footers. Three narrow aisles intersected the desks. There were short desks for one pupil, each at the wall and two longer ones between, seating two pupils each. Attached to the front row of desks were recitation seats. All the seats and desks were roughly built of heavy pine planks, once bare and plain, but with the years, adorned with drawing of houses and animals, ink spots and the "jack knife's carved initial." Beneath each desk was a shelf for books and personal belongings.

At the back, a plank seat built against the wall, reached the width of the room, on which sat the largest boys and girls at their desks. For the greater needs of those older pupils, an additional shelf was placed beneath the seat. The long shelf under the seat, on the boy's side, possessed possibilities not intended by the builder. When the shelf was moved up and down, the ends rubbing against the supports of the seat, gave forth a baleful groan. The musical instrument could be operated by the calf of the leg, while the performer's two hands conspicuously held his geography; and his innocent and studious gaze was fixed upon its pages. Years after, in my sophomore night duties, I learned of the value of rosin rubbed on the plank of the "devil's fiddle." Much we might have added to the pitch and tone of that shelf, if a piece of rosin had been a part of the equipment of mischief. But without that improvement, the shelf was thought worthy to be tried on every new teacher. I can see now the startled, astonished, sometimes frightened look, of a new teacher at the first low moan swelling to a hoarse bellow; and signaling the rear rows to be very silent and studious, while the little ones giggled and glanced knowingly at the puzzled teacher.

At the centre of the open space in front of the lines of desks stood a huge box stove, from which a funnel rose almost to the ceiling and ran back, to enter the chimney at the rear of the room. The object of this long funnel, I suppose was economy of heat. But it was apt to smoke in bad weather. Then what coughing, sneezing and weeping ensued. Sometimes when skating was very good, a few handfuls of wet pine needles dropped skillfully down the chimney to lodge in the funnel, would secure for us a much-desired holiday. The stove stood upon four long legs above a big piece of zinc. Under the stove, the boys and girls deposited their dinner pails and boxes to keep them warm.

It was a great grief to me that I could have no dinner pail to place under the stove with the others, to glance at with pleasant anticipation during the forenoon. Unhappily, my home was only a few rods distance from the school-house and when the others at noon, sat down in pleasant groups around the stove and on the benches and opened their pails, I had to run home and take my place at the family diner table. There I gulped my dinner in the shortest time possible and rushed back to school, to lose the fewest precious minutes of the noon play hour. There were other hardships in living so near the school house. The teacher usually boarder at our house, which sometimes estranged me from my mates. Sometimes, usually without reason, I was looked upon as the recipient of favors from the "teacher's partiality." My mother promised me that any punishment received at school should be visited on me in double measure at home, and Mother always kept her word. Some of my inflictions at school might have been entrusted to my forgetfulness, but for the teacher's habit of reviewing the events of the school day in the home circle. After many days, came to me a great reward for hardships patiently borne as a result of the teacher's living at our home. I came home on one of my last college vacations to find sitting opposite me at the table a fair faced, laughing-eyed, sweet voiced, young school teacher who – but all of that belongs in the chapters of a later biography that will never be written.[3]

On the walls hung small outline maps that interested me, although few teachers seemed to know how to make any use of them, or the globe that stood in the alcove. On each side of the room, fastened to the wall, was a small wooden blackboard on which we "did our sums," and wrote our sentences with lumps of chalk. For school crayons had not yet been invented. Each pupil brought from home a piece of cloth for an eraser, and often the collection looked as if it taken from Joseph's worn-out coat. In the corner on a low shelf, hovered over by clouds of chalk dust, stood an open pail of drinking water, with a battered tin dipper hanging from a nail above it.

With all its crudeness and meagerness of furnishings, Pleasant Valley school-house had a rough comfort and a wholesome healthfulness. We did not need bubble fountains, for the doctors had not yet invented microbes to colonize our open water pail and common drinking cup. The pupils loyally did all they could to make us comfortable. At four o'clock each afternoon, we had put away our books and made ready for closing; the master would say, "Whose turn it is?" A boy and a girl would raise their right hands. The boy thus pledged himself, to lock the school-house, take home the ponderous key, and next morning return and build the fire. He might live two or three miles away, and have many chores to do night and morning, but it was a point of honor to build the fire on the shortest and coldest morning in season and to have the room as comfortable as it could be made at nine o'clock, with armfuls of wood piled under the west blackboard sufficient for the day. The girl who had raised her hand, promised to devote her noon hour next day, to sweeping out and dusting the school-room and she did her task as faithfully as her brother.

Rough and unlovely as was our school-house and its furnishings, no school in New England today, has so beautiful a school grounds as District Number Six possessed. We were unhampered by fences, as to bounds none knew where they were. A level grassy plain stretched away on three sides. Two enormous pine trees stood close together on the east side of the house, in whose great branches we rigged a swing and entertained the girls with awkward but well-meant gallantry. At the back of the school-house, was an extensive grove of intermingled hard and soft pine trees, giants every one. Who had the forethought to save this bit of the primeval forests, the pride and joy of pleasant valley, we never knew. The last of those noble trees bowed to the needs of the modern school years ago. But the scent of the pines with the hot sun upon them, the cool breeze that swept through their shaded aisles, the sighing of waving boughs, the tread of he pine needles under my feet are with me still. In the sunny space to the south of the grove grew great patches of wild strawberries, the biggest sweetest, wild berries ever found. In their shadows to the north, the lady slippers stole up through the yellow carpet of needles and waved at us their purple buskins[4]. The robins always nested in the branches of the smaller trees within reach of our curiosity. In the tops of the tallest trees, a small colony of crows kept house. Their noisy gossip came in to us through the open windows as we sat at our books. We heard, in the hot sunshine outside, the snapping and whirring of the grasshopper's wings, the chirping of the crickets, the locusts stabbing the drowsy silence of the room.

At recess in the grove we watched the vast armies of aphids moving in perfect alignment, rank on rank, millions of them, no stragglers, no halts, marching slowly down the bark of one tree across a bit of ground and up the trunk of another at the command of some unseen commander-in-chief, what were they? Whence came they? Wither they going?

In the grove, we laid out houses of many apartments, defined by windrows of pine needless. And there, the girls kept house with bits of broken china and received, with stately grace, on smooth hard floors of sand clean swept of every falling leaf. We had a circus ring, round which we road bare-back our imaginary horses, and did our stunts of acrobatic wonders. In the tree trunks, we cut little reservoirs to catch the amber drops of pitch, and when they were full set fire to the contents to make from the residue a chewing gum, with a flavor that Wrigley's has never attained. We played games: "Hook Sticks[5]", "Tag my Goal", "Three and Four Old Cat[6]", "Snap the Whip[7]", all games that passed with the school house and great trees. I never see children play them now.

Under the ancient educational system, the towns of Massachusetts were divided into school districts. Each district furnished a lot, erected and kept in repair the school house. At an annual school meeting, it elected a prudential school committeeman to look after the material interests of the district and nominate the teachers for the ensuing year, subject to the decision of the "examining" committee whose examinations were more often formalities, but sometimes veritable "third degrees". I remember going out from an interview with an examining committee filled with rage at their inexcusable and indelicate curiosity in regard to my age and attainments. The examining committee was elected at the annual town meeting, usually the doctor, minister, or lawyer, men of education, competent to examine candidates for teaching and to be responsible for the mental progress of the school.

We had two terms of school, a summer and a winter, each of about twelve weeks. The summer term was attended by the little children and taught by young girls, mere tyros[8] who had just attained to the dignity of long skirts. The winter term was taught by a man, usually a college undergraduate. The New England colleges used to provide a long winter vacation and adjustment of studies, so that needy men could go out for a term of teaching. Many college students taught winter schools for the experience, and they usually got a great deal out of it. Such a system gave to a district a different teacher almost every term.

The schools in the rural districts were known as "ungraded," which they surely were, particularly in the winter term. There were always more classes than individual pupils. In our school, the subjects ranged from the alphabet to higher arithmetic, algebra, Latin and occasionally a student in metaphysics, under the name of Mental Philosophy. To d ecline to teach any subject was evidence of incapacity. And, it must be all accomplished in a school day of six hours, with two noisy, distracting recesses of ten minutes in the midst of each session and an intermission of an hour at noon. Add to this the duty of maintaining order among a throng ebullient with mischief and the answering of thousands of questions the ingenuity of bright and restless children can devise. But it as only pure unmalicious mischief, that our teachers had to encounter. Our big boys were gentlemen and the girls, ladies. There was no disposition to initiate new teachers with a rough house; no talk of throwing the master or the stove out-of-doors. If the teacher were competent, tactful, possessed of humor, which means understanding of human nature, and in earnest, as he usually is, he had the love and loyal support of us all.

Our schoolroom originally furnished accommodations, such as they were, for thirty-six pupils. At the opening of the winter term in my day, sixty, sometimes seventy pupils presented themselves for enrollment. The problem of providing for so many called for tact, ingenuity, and patience with great resourcefulness, as the district treasury was always empty. The winter I began my school career, Father was the prudential committee and had to solve a very grave problem of seating with an empty district treasury. He made from rough planks, long low benches to stand around the open space at the front of the room thus seating a lot of little chaps. By good fortune, George Russell and I were assigned to a very short bench made to fit into the corner by the water pail. We always read and recited out number lessons the first thing in the morning and for the rest of the long forenoon were left to our own devices. In the middle of our seat, we discovered a large augur hole which we converted into a grist mill. Gathering handfuls of dust and bits of chalk from the blackboards we poured them down through our mill again and again grinding grists through many happy hours. Desiring to expand our business, I filled my pocket one morning with kernels of corn and took them to school. After reciting our lesson, we were very eager to grind out new grist. We dropped a few kernels cautiously down through the mill. Then something happened. There was a hole in the floor under the shelf of the water pail. Out of the hole darted a squirrel, seized a kernel of our corn, and whisked back again. Two shrieks of delighted laughter, two excited youngsters leaping into the aisle riveted the attention of the entire school upon our corner. There was a dreadful pause of expectant suspense as the teacher laid down his book and approached us. There was no time for investigation of for making allowance for an extraordinary circumstance. The two little millers, each by the convenient hand of an ear, were led away to the opposite corner to stand and repent until noon.

It was fortunate for me to begin my school days in the winter term. School opened on the first Monday in December 1857 or '58 it must have been. A new light snow fall glittering in the winter sunshine made fairyland of fields and woods as, holding tight to her hand, I set out with my sister, nine years my senior, for the school house. How carefully that morning and ever after 'till I reached years of discretion, my sister watched over my steps that harm might not come to body, mind, or soul. Dear Sister, very beautiful in face and form and innocent, guileless soul; perhaps you did not know why we were greeted so cordially at the school house that winter morning; why your little brother was so kindly treated by the big boys; why they asked him to coast with them on their fastest sleds; why they filled his pockets with the choicest nuts and apples; why the young school masters never had a textbook of their own but sat always down by your side to look over yours while you read your Latin.

My memory of that day is, I suppose, a composite of the pictures of many school days. Just before nine o'clock, the master enters with brisk step his fine face aglow from the frosty air. He nods pleasantly to the groups standing around the stove and stuffs in a couple of logs, pushes three or four projecting dinner pails father under the stove and seizes the big bell from his desk. In response to the vigorous ringing, from the grove, from the snow banks behind the shed, from the colossus in snow that they are building across the road, the pupils come trooping in. What a blowing of clouds of steam into the frosty air! What stamping of feet in the entry where stands the master wielding the broom to brush off the clinging snow from clothing and clumsy boots. We give each other last punches, pokes and kicks of good camaraderie and hurry to our seats.

The master, and he is the master of the situation, gravely seats himself behind his desk. We open our testaments. It is the turn of the second two read this morning. We always begin on the girl's side. A tall, angular girl in the wall seat rises, paling and flushing. There are some hard words in the first verse of the tenth chapter of John[9]. But, with an occasional lift from the teacher, Lucinda stumbles through and sinks relieved into her seat as the next girl rises. After the last boy in the row has read we close out testaments and all bow our heads reverently on our hands with our fingers adjusted for an occasional peak, we all repeat with the master the Lord's Prayer. Our devotions are very brief perhaps seem hurried. But the devout worshipping, believing spirit of our teacher impresses us. The memory of those few minutes will help us to keep our faith in God in the stress of life.

Now the business of the morning session begins. The tots gather about the teacher's knee; with pencil pointing to the open page of the primer, he impresses upon them that the very crooked letter is S and the straight one is I; another group a size larger follows to read "go up, go on, go on up". Then five or six of us draw near with out Emerson's *Arithmetic*[10]. For five minutes, we discuss animatedly the ever shifting groups of restless blackbirds alighting on the bars of the farm gate.

But now attention must be given to the distress signals of upraised hands flying all over the room. Jamie is thirsting for a drink of water. Five boys hold up dripping slates. Desirous to begin the day with clean slates they have drenched them with a bottle of water kept for that purpose. They must go to the stove and dry their slates before they can "do their sums". Luella wishes to come and sit on the step of the alcove to warm her feet. The controversy arising from too warm an exchange of spit balls across the middle aisle must be settled. The six children around the stove push and jostle and kick the dinner pails beneath. One heats his slate till it cracks and the wood frame of another slate takes fire. All of these diversions must be instantly and amenably settled as the work goes pretty steady on.

Now a file of boys and girls marches out and lines with toes on a crack of a long board on the west side of the stove. It is the fourth class in spelling with Sarah at the head and Joe at the foot. These are always the positions of Sarah and Joe. Every Monday morning the law requires Sarah to take her place at the foot of the class to give others a chance and show her smartness in working back again. At the first round, she goes above Joe, and by Tuesday, Sarah is in her old proud place again.

After recess come the more advanced arithmetic classes and the algebra. The last three minutes of the morning session must be given to Rosman who is studying Greenleaf's *National Arithmetic*[11], a big thick book bound in black. At the end are twenty pages of miscellaneous examples and they are "awful examples" every one. That big square shouldered boy in the back corner seat with the splendid white teeth and deep base voice is of senior wrangler. With almost no help from the teacher, he will solve every one of those examples this winter.

This afternoon session is more enjoyed by everybody. After the play of the noon hour, we are all in the mood for quiet study. The school-room clean, swept, and dusted, the renewed fire crackling and snapping in the big stove, the winter sunshine streaming in through the western windows makes a pleasant cheerful setting.

The first thing on the afternoon program is reading all the older pupils Sargent's *Fifth Reader*[12]. Many are excellent reader and furnish to us young listeners a fine entertainment. Many of us, I am sure, developed a taste for good literature by listening in school to the reading of the well chosen selections of English Classics contained in the series of school readers edited by Epes Sargent.

As the *National Arithmetic* was the pride of the morning session, session, the class in Analysis and Parsing[13] was the glory of the afternoon. It was impressive and exhilarating to see all the young men and women moving up to assemble at the front of the room routing out the occupants of the front seats to find place where they might. That recitation almost rivaled in interest for me my sister's Latin which came last in the afternoon. It was so exciting when some young man ventured to differ with the teacher on the disposal of a word or the meaning of a verse in Gray's *Elegy*[14], and others joined in a warm discussion, talking right out in school. And sitting there winter after winter with wide open eager ears, I learned by a kind of absorption English grammar, analysis and parsing, and when they came to us a regular study, it was no big bear or stumbling block to any of us. Today, in our schools, Grammar is a word to be uttered with bated breath. Sugar-coated, predigested substitutes are administered in place of it. Consequently, pupils cannot speak or write good English and do not recognize good English when they read it because they are ignorant of the fundamental laws of the language.

Sometimes we looked out the west window at Dr. Huse's white horse and red cutter[15] coming down the village road. The village doctor[16] was our Examining Committee. As he dashed around the corner of the house and tied and blanketed the horse at the big pipe, play subsided, faces sobered, bodies straightened, neglected books were resumed and solemn stillness brooded over the room as the doctor entered, We all resolve to do our level best for the sake of the teacher and the honor of Pleasant Valley. But the visits of the Examination Committee were never an ordeal. At four o'clock, we laid aside our books, folded our arms, and listened to the doctor's kindly, helpful, generally commendatory speech.

We long remembered the close of one. The doctor turned to an urchin on the long bench saying, "and when I come next time I will bring a quieting pill for Charley". We were very eager for the next visit to see what Charley's pill would look like and how it would affect him. I think the doctor forgot to bring the pill. But it would affect no cure. Blue-eyed, curly haired, laughing Charley was always getting himself and his neighbors into a scrape, a scamp in his school days, a scoundrel in his mature life.

Shortly after the close of the Civil War, our town established a high school and placed in charge of it a young graduate of Colby. He organized the motley material offered into three classes, the youngest of which I joined. For a year and a half, night and morning, I walked the three miles between home and school. At the last bend of the road before entering the village, I used to pause under a great willow, to draw out from its hiding place in the wall, my primitive dressing case, an old blacking brush, a comb and a corn broom, and primp up to a state worthy of urban streets and the dignity of a high school student. There were several other farm boys, like myself walking daily, many miles from the remote parts of town. It was soon manifest, that the boys and girls from the ungraded rural schools were as well-prepared to do high school work as the pupils from the graded, all-year-round schools of the village. The long walks were no detriment to us, save in the loss of precious time. We did not need the gymnasium we helped set up in the high school attic.

So, for a year and a half, I went and came between home and school, did my farm chores night, morning and Saturdays. Meanwhile, the enthusiasm of our scholarly principal had crystallized into a definite purpose in my mind, the vague thoughts of college. One Saturday afternoon late in the fall, Father and I had been to the village with "Pony" on some errand. Returning, we met the chairman of the school board, who at once stated his business. He was in need of a teacher to teach the winter school in the Bartlett District on the other side of the town, and offered me the position, saying he though I was competent and would succeed, if I could conceal the fact that I was but sixteen years of age. I was a well grown boy, square shouldered and well set-up. Moreover, I had upon each cheek a few carefully nurtured, pale, downy hairs, which I hastened that very afternoon, to have dyed a definite brown, and spoke of them openly as "side whiskers"

Monday morning, in a rage snow storm, fortified by my whiskers and a resolute purpose, I presented myself at the Bartlett School and began my teaching. The building was a tumble down shell, in the corner of a field with no pine grove or other pleasant surroundings. It seemed to me, that the students were very inferior to those I had played and studied with in Pleasant Valley. There were a good many large boys and girls. But they seemed to study my whiskers more than their books. But I did my best and at the end of term, the committee, and several of the parents, told me I had made good.

One pupil, I became deeply interested in and felt much satisfaction in his remarkable progress. He was an ex-slave[17], a man probably forty years of age. He was the last of the slaves to be set free, wandered north to our town and got an opportunity to work for board and go to school in the Bartlett district. It was with a strange feeling at first, that I taught that man, a mature man in body, but a very little child in mind, to read. I always stood holding the primer toward him, pointing out the letters, his coal-black face alight with eagerness, the great pathetic eyes following every move of my pencil, the thick lips repeating the letters in a soft drawl, the wooly head twisting from side to side to fix more firmly in his mind, their shapes. We began the study of numbers at the same time. I found he could count to about twenty. Oh, the astonishing progress the negro made! Many times a day, I looked at that absorbed figure in the back row, utterly lost to his surroundings, his head bent low over his slate, counting his additions and subtractions on his scrawny black fingers and carefully setting down results. When examination day came, the negro was my star pupil, reading with intelligence, almost fluency and working correctly, an example in simple interest. I wish I might know something of the man's later life.

I went back to the high school for but a single term. Father's health was breaking down and the farm help was hard to obtain. So I had to leave school and take up the work in the barn and the fields. But I could not relinquish my plan for college. A little time for study was found and occasionally, I walked to the village in the evening and recited to the high school principal. But the village road at night was long and lonely.

I began to think of Phillips Andover Academy which was only eight miles distant. Could I not enter the Middle Class in the spring, and complete my preparation in four terms of that famous fitting school? One afternoon late in the fall, I went to Andover to consult the Principal in regard to my plan. Dr. Samuel H. Taylor[18] was a famous teacher of the old school. He taught directly only the Senior Class. The students who met him in the classroom came to admire and love their great teacher. To others he was a stern martinet.

I rang Dr. Taylor's bell almost hoping to find he was not at home. But I was at once ushered into his study. Dr. Taylor was sitting in an arm chair, I think, by an open fire. As I entered, he fixed a penetrating look on me throughout his hold rimmed glasses and without rising or offering his hand, motioned me to the chair and waited for me to state my errand. In tones that I knew trembled, I told him of my wish to enter the Middle Class in the Spring. With a few rapid questions, he leaned how much I had done and of my study by myself. He then told me I had covered quite as much ground as the class but probably not thoroughly: that

I must enter the school at once. I said that, owing to the conditions at home, it was impossible. At that point, a student entered the room to whom the Doctor turned, allowing me to withdraw without another word.

I never saw Doctor Taylor again. A few months later, one Sunday morning, as he was entering the Academy to meet his Bible class, the summons came. He fell on the stairs and died, a man a little past the prime of life wearing the harness of a great responsibility. I have always greatly regretted that my one personal impression and memory of one of the greatest educators of New England of the nineteenth century and kindliest of men should be such as it was.

In that discouraging interview, Dr. Taylor mentioned a book he had just published "*Aids to Classical Study*[19]" which would help me. Before I left Andover that afternoon, I went to Mr. Draper's bookstore[18], and inquiring the price, found it to be exactly the amount I had in my pocket including the cost of my return ticket. I bought the book and walked home to find Father and Mother very anxious over my long absence and the unfed cows awaiting me with clashing horns down the stanchion row.

It was a long, hard, grinding winter for the farm boy. Father was too ill to do anything but sit despondently in the house. The care of the animals and the preparing of the next seasons wood filled the house of the brief winter days. When I sat down to my books, I was too sleepy and tired for study. Then I adopted a plan of study that in times of pressure I have found useful all of my life. I sent my mental dial to three, sometimes two-o'clock in the morning, got up at that hour and dressed. Bitterly cold were the creaking back stairs and the long kitchen as I went down to build a fire in the living room. I was soon at my books. When it was time to light the lantern and go to the barn, I had secured several hours of clear-headed uninterrupted study.

Then, after I had done up all the morning work, how good Mother's substantial, hot breakfast tasted.

The "*Aids to Classical Study*" proved to be of great value to me. It consisted of short selections from the text of the Greek and Latin Classics commonly read in preparation for college. On these selections were based hundreds of questions on grammar, history, mythology, geography, every conceivable phase of classical study. There were references to many books I did not possess and could not afford to buy. Questions I could not answer I marked and, making an occasional extra trip to the village, I looked them up in our minister's extensive library. Page upon page of Harkness' *Latin Grammar with Rules and their Exceptions*[20], I learned and recited to the cows as I milked them. One morning the following winter at a Latin recitation in Phillips Academy, we had an interested visitor, a small pleasant faced man. After the recitation, the teacher called me to the desk and introduced me to Professor Harkness[21], as the boy who knew his *Latin Grammar* from cover to cover. It was a very exaggerated statement, but I did not tell Professor Harkness that I owed the thoroughness of what I did know, to the milking stool.

And the daily tasks of the farm were drilled into my mind just as lastingly as rules of syntax. Often and often all my life I have dreamed of going to the old barn to find the neglected cows waiting to be milked and fed. So the long winter of 1871 passed. With the coming Spring, Father's health improved. Everything looked brighter with the season of budding hope. When I went again to Andover, I found the academy in the temporary charge of Professor Goldsmith[22]. A talk with several of the teachers resulted in my being permitted to join tentatively a second division of the Middle Class made up of boys who had been in the school a shorter time than the majority of the class. However, it was predicted that I would be unable to keep up.

What Phillipian of fifty years ago does not remember the two rows of small three story wooden dormitories fringing the old Campus known as English and Latin Commons? I was assigned to Room 4 in the first house of Latin Commons. The rooms were let to students unfurnished and without heat or light.

The afternoon before the opening of school, Father and I loaded the farm wagon with dry wood from the shed, tied on the few room furnishings I had been able to get together, and set out for Andover. On the way, Father told me that he and Mother would help me all they could to get through the Academy, if I could finish in four terms. Then I must give up all the idea of college and come home to help on the farm.

Arriving at the Academy, I saw with burning cheeks that our queer outfit was an object of amused curiosity to the nattily dressed students lounging around the doors of Latin Commons; the clumsy farm horse with a halter large as a cable around her neck, the springless blue farm wagon, the unusual birch wood, the old fashioned furniture. As we carried the furniture upstairs to my room, through open doors of other rooms, I got glimpses of pretty carpets, easy chairs, pictures on the walls. After bidding goodbye to Father, I went back to my room and my belongings; two chairs, a small unpainted table, a wall bookcase I had made, a small stove my sister had given to me, a narrow bed with a straw filled tick, three small braided rugs Mother had insisted on my taking for my bare, unpainted floor, and a lamp. These I had disposed as effectively as I could, built a fire and say down at my small study table. A great fear took possession of me, a fear that with my home-made, ill fitting clothes, a poor bare room, I should be regarded by those with whom I was to mingle as different - that difference summer up in a single terrible word - COUNTRYFIED.

It was with a sinking heart, that I head the school bell calling me to the first recitation the following afternoon. The lesson was the first eight or ten verses of the Aeneid. I had prepared it with the utmost care. The teacher of the second division of the Middle Class that term was Dr. Hawkes. Shortly after the beginning of the recitation, he called me up. I rose with shaking knees and translated the verses indicated correctly, I think. Then Dr. Hawkes began asking questions. They were the very ones asked in the "*Aids*". Prompt correct answers led to more, till he had fired at me a perfect fusillade of questions. The pleased glance toward me as he said, "that will do" did not escape me. I trod on air as I went back to my room. I had "rushed" my first recitation in Phillips Academy.

As the term went on, I perceived I had little to fear in the recitations in the Classics. Because I had had nothing like the "*Aids*" to help me in Mathematics, I never was able to make good that deficiency. I found, too, that my classmates gave no heed to my ill fitting clothes or poor bare room but took me for what I was honestly trying to be. In the Phillips Academy of fifty years ago as well as of today, a boy passed current for that he really was, for what he was honestly trying to make of himself.

A year later I was able to graduate sixth in a class of fifty four boys, most of whom had enjoyed from the beginning the splendid drill of the Academy classrooms. It was a great encouragement to the farm boy, who had worked so much alone.

One undertaking of my senior year proved to be of much importance to my future. The Means Prize for Original Declamations[24] had recently been established. I spent much time and toil on my composition. It was accepted and after the competition in the school hall, It was announced that I was the winner of the first prize. I well remember that, as I retired from the stage, after receiving my prize, I saw not the great audience, not my applauding class mates, not even the Fem Sems[25] who had honored us by their presence in a body, but only Father, Mother and Sister and from the look on Father's face I knew that I could go to college.

"Here now the substance of the whole matter," saith the prophet. I very well know that the school systems of today, urban and rural alike, are greatly superior to anything we were able to enjoy. Yet I know also that the old time, ungraded, district school with its necessity for forbearance, good example, and protection on the part of older pupils toward the little ones, the opportunity of younger to look up to, hear and see the progress of the elders, was a great force for the making of manhood and womanhood. Our small boys were always full of mischief but it was unmalicious, unresentful, pure mischief. Our big boys were always gentlemen, our girls, ladies, the teachers of our winter terms were competent, tactful, and in earnest and almost invariably possessed the love and loyalty of us all.

If I had painted the picture of the old school among the great trees in Pleasant Valley in too bright colors, attribute the failing to old eyes grown misty with recalling pleasant scenes long past, merry voices long silent.

VII. The Extension Courses of District Number Six.

The school house in Pleasant Valley was the center of all our interests. Here we met for our few evening gatherings. The room had no provisions for lighting, but every responsible adult brought a candle and candlestick or, when whale oil and kerosene came on the market, a hand lamp. These, when lighted and distributed around on desks and window ledges, made the room bright and cheery.

The opportunities offered for general improvement where the Spelling School, the Singing School, Major Little's Concerts, and the school library. All of them except the library were very popular.

The Spelling School on Friday nights crowded the house to the doors. All the pupils and nearly all the grown-ups of the district attended. At half-past seven, the master called the meeting to order and asked for nominations for leaders of the spelling match. George Gage and my sister, Jennie, were usually selected. They then took their stations in the two outer aisles at the back of the room and proceeded to the selection of the other contestants. To the lady belongs the first choice. With a thrill of delight, I hear my sister's low clear voice calling my name. My sister always called me first. She knew it was a stimulus to the little boy's ambition and I could spell. We gave much thought to spelling at home, were always challenging each other to spell words at the table and looking up new words in the dictionary. It was grand to stand on tiptoe next to Sister, look up into her face, and resolve to fight the battle to the last ditch.

It is now George Gage's choice and he calls Elvira Russell. She is the best speller in the school and there are other obvious reasons why George likes to have Elvira stand next to him. The selection goes rapidly on. It is customary to invite everybody to participate. All the pupils and a goodly number of the older people accept till to opposing lines stand facing each other down the aisles clear across the room into the alcove. The master now takes his station in front of the stove. We appoint no referee. Public sentiment expressed in low groans or applause will be final arbiter. The master runs his fingers through his hair, clears his throat, and opens the speller almost at the first page. It is an unwritten law that we shall spell round once with unbroken ranks and no disasters even if we have to resort to such words as cat and hen. It is terrible when, on the first round, big, blundering, red-headed Sherb spells horse, H-O-R-S–, and then is stuck. No punching from his neighbors, no groans, or wide mouthed signals from the audience can spur the frightened boy to add the -e. In disgrace, Sherb slinks back to his seat.

With the second round, the words grow harder and the weak ones begin to fall. Round after round we toss the words back and forth, the master working toward the last page of the speller and the ranks growing thinner and thinner. "Lovable," a very simple word but with the horrid truck of dropping the "e" after "v" proves my Waterloo. The last page of the speller is reached and exhausted. Elvira Russell on the other side like the Secretary stands along. Sister and Clarence Walton survive on our side. The master draws from his pocket his private list of annihilators. Elvira goes down on "ratiocination." Sister stumbles over "syzygy[1]", leaving little white haired Clarence Walton (he is a sugar baron in Hawaii now) sole survivor and our side is pronounced victorious.

After the intermission, during which many apples, nuts and cornballs[2] are dispensed, a curtain is stretched across the alcove and a "lyceum program" is staged. First, the curtain swings aside revealing Sherb in wide rimmed slouch hat, a basket on his arm, kneeling on the floor, and fishing in a pond in front of the stove. Roosman enters and asks, "get any bites?" "yep," "Where? under your hat?" And Rossman flees pursued by the infuriated fisherman. Next I declaim "Excelsior[3]" and am followed by Fred Russell with "Casabianca.[4]" Then comes a dialogue well acted by several of the older boys and girls.

Meanwhile, out in the entry we are treating Eugene Kimball's face with burnt cork and broadening the expanse of his lips with red chalk.[5] As he enters, rolling his big black eyes and revealing generously his handsome teeth, we all realize Nature's mistake in making Eugene white. Bur, alas, we have forgotten to treat his left hand with the cork, an omission that becomes glaringly apparent as he flourishes his fists in the stump speech.

But there could be nothing finer than Willard Carlton's rendering of Dr. Holmes's "September Gale."[6] Big broad shouldered, deep chested, splendid fellow, how we laughed when he announced in the first line, "I'm not a chicken." And the pathos in his deep bass voice, as he bewailed his little pantaloons straddling through the air and borne away on the wild gale.

Out of the good natured competition, the excitement, the fun, the efforts of the performers, the applause of the audience, the Spelling School brought discipline and entertainment in the dull winter months.

My memory of the Singing School, which alternated on Friday nights with the Spelling School, is not vivid. Perhaps I was not equally interested. I had no ear for music, and made poor progress in learning to read it or to sing. I have, however, one clear memory picture, of the master standing before the black board, a lighted candle in his left hand, a lump of chalk and an eraser cloth in his right, his pitch pipe between his teeth like a cigarette, talking rapidly, and a little incoherently, on account of the pipe, about the musical staff, lines, spaces, clefs, half notes, quarter notes. Nothing of which, could I get clear in my mind. My thoughts would wander away to Monday's arithmetic lesson or to wonder whether I could pluck courage enough (I never did but once) to ask Sarah Gage if I might see her home after school. However, not all the boys shared my ill success either with the staff or Sarah. In after years, in the church choirs of Boston, and the concert halls of the country were heard voices that were first attuned in the Singing School of Pleasant Valley.

Sometimes, usually late in the fall, a modest little handbill would be left at every home in the Valley announcing that Monday evening next Major Alfred Little[7] would give a concert in the School. The world everywhere esteems a man who lives a brave, cheerful, useful life under the handicap of some great physical disability. Major Little was a helpless cripple. In infancy, apparently some paralysis had caused his lower limbs to wither. His feet were not larger than those of a Chinese lady of quality[8]. Bit his body, arms and head where those of a large stalwart man. His large face framed in a long, silken, yellow beard ever wore a bright, cheery look and his high dome-like forehead and fine eyes betokened a scholarly intelligence.

He was a composer of music and played and sang beautifully. He had invented and built with his own hand a wonderful musical instrument adapted to his limitations. Its bellows were activated by his elbows leaving his hands and wrists free for the keys[9].

On the evening of the concert, the Major would arrive in a democrat wagon[10] seated on the trunk containing his wonderful musical instrument. He was tenderly lifted from the wagon and carried into the school house by strong and willing hands. Father and I had already carried over from our house a certain stout table and a tall light stand for which loam the price of our admission which was ten cents was scrupulously remitted to us. Once just before the beginning of a concert, I found a little maiden weeping bitterly in the entry. She had lost or forgotten to bring her money. Since I was to go in dead head, I proposed to loan of my dime which the little girl reluctantly accepted by insisted that I keep her small red mittens as security till such time as her father could pay her debt. The house was always crowded and the proceeds of the concert quiet a pocketful of dimes.

At the word of command we would seat the major on the table, put his trunk beneath for his little feet to rest upon, place his instrument on the light stand before him, and all was then in readiness. With his elbows and forearms pressing alternately on the ends he locked the musical cradle and pumped the bellows full.

"Ladies and Gentlemen, I will now play 'Pleasant Valley Quick Step, No. 4'. It has never been played before and never will again". and out of that queer, careening, mahogany box under the Major's flying fingers would pour such a flood of merry, rollicking music as only Major Little could compose. Presently the musician's clear tenor voice would sound out above the road of the instrument, singing verses and music improvised as in the old troubadour days, celebrating the loveliness of Pleasant Valley, the charm of it women, the valor of its men. Oh, how very wonderful and inspiring it was to us all.

The subsequent numbers were less exciting, patriotic songs, love ditties, selections from operas, beautifully rendered, sometimes he added the songs of sweet voiced children he had trained. So, for two happy hours, Major Alfred Little's concert held us delighted, entranced. Laugh not! the example of the cheerful, patient, brave life of that helpless man, his rollicking music that we could understand were, to us of simple ways, worth more than the finest symphony concert.

Once, when at play in my uncle's attic, I came upon a small red cupboard marked "School Library". Its shelves were filled with nearly covered, carefully labeled books. I learned at home that several years before a sum of money had been raised in some way, a hundred books purchased and my uncle made librarian. But people were too busy to read and presently the library was quite forgotten. To me it was buried treasure and I hastened to dig it up. There were histories of Greece, Rome, England and America in many volumes; several works of Mental and Moral Science whose repose I never disturbed; and the chief treasure of the old cupboard, a complete set of the Rollo Books[11]. For two or three years I went and came to my uncle's attic, devouring those books in a long feast, as the last of the extension course at District Number Six enrolled its solitary student.

IIIV. The Yellow Rose Bush

Pleasant Valley was fortunate in being served by two practitioners, the Old Doctor, and the Young Doctor. Young Doctor was only a relative term, for Young Doctor was a gray-haired, bent, old man as long ago as I can remember. An always pleasant sight was the Young Doctor with a light pick over his shoulder, a basket on his arm, hunting along the brooks and over the hills for simples. For the Doctors depended upon roots and herbs for healing. Both Doctors were men of the kindliest hearts and for many years helped us much in our troubles.

Very late in life, Old Doctor married a second time, a woman many years her junior. The new Mrs. Old Doctor was a bustling energetic woman and a spiritualistic medium of high potential. She interested the Valley in Spiritualism. For several years Saturday evening séances were held in the darkened kitchen of Old Doctor's home. Often times the spirit of a very ancient Indian medicine man was invoked and gave, through the medium, invaluable information as to when and where to find roots and herbs of hitherto unknown efficacy; and so our homeopaths, allopaths and herbipaths.

But the Young Doctor's greatest medical discovery was made not by help from the spirit world, rather by merest accident. One Spring, Young Doctor went to his herb attic over the woodshed to find that his stock was practically exhausted, only leaves, roots and stems scattered on the floor, and further to discover where the white turkey had stolen her nest and hatched her turklings. In his need, young Doctor swept up clean the floor with the egg hulls and other foreign matter, steeped the contents of the dust-pan and added Medford rum[1]. The compound proved to be a powerful "exlir" especially valuable in cases of chronic "dyspepsie".

In Old Doctor's Meadow opposite our lower mowing field stood a wide spreading, noble oak. One night word came from the spirit world that a great treasure, a wash boiler filled with gold coins was buried under the oak. The news naturally created great excitement in Pleasant Valley. In was soon resolved that all hands should get together the next Saturday afternoon and exhume the boiled. Father would lend no countenance to such an enterprise and Mother was indignant that I was allowed to share in it. Right after I shouldered my shovel, a small urchin for much shoveling but big enough to bring home a share of the gold, and set out for the oak tree.

Most of the men folks and all the boy folks of the Valley were there. To make the finding of the treasure doubly sure we marked out a very large circle round the tree. Roots and stones made the digging very hard at first. But later we came to a white sand and went down faster, everyone eager to be first to strike his shovel on the cover of the boiler. But before that occurred six o'clock came. There were supper and milking, so we decided to exhume the boiler later and went home. On Sunday came the startling news that somebody in the night had dug down further and carried off the treasure. An investigating committee hurried to the spot and later reported that more sand evidently had been thrown out and that there was a broad mark across the sand as though a thick plank or bottom of a heavy wash boiler had been dragged over it.

In the high winds of the next winter, the noble old oak toppled over and died. We never saw the color of the money in the wash boiler. Bit the thought of those broad hold pieces reminds me of the gold disks that used to unfold of the great yellow rose bush under the window of Mother's room.

For several years when I was a small boy, the Catholic Churches of Haverhill maintained a mission in the younger city of Lawrence. Every week a priest from Haverhill rode by on his duties in Lawrence. He was a man of noble bearing, as my childish eyes could see, a refined and polished gentlemen. Mother was Scotch Irish blood from the North of Ireland, and the Battle of the Boyne would boil at the sight of the stranger and her tongue tell of the dark deeds of the older faith, till I came to regard the man as a dangerous monster.

On a June day when the yellow rose bush was in its glory and I was absorbed in play near it, I heard a refined voice say, "Little boy is your mother at home?" There was that terrible man mounted on his high horse right beside me! Without waiting to reply, I made for the house. "Mother, that awful priest is right here in our yard and he is asking for your!" I expected to see Mother rush to bolt the doors and hide me under her bed. Instead, she calmly slipped off her apron and hastened to the door. After an exchange of greetings as affable on Mother's part as the priest's, he asked if he might have some yellow roses which Mother began to gather without the least hesitation. The monster then dismounted, threw the rein over the hitching post, and advanced close up to Mother. Soon they were walking up and down the garden paths together, Mother and that priest, talking only as mutual lovers of flowers in a blooming garden can do. I never heard Mother speak harshly of the priest after that day and her strictures on his religion grew gradually less severe. But she had to hear a great deal from Father about propaganda and proselytizing although he did not use those terms. But the hour of Father's downfall was drawing on and by the agency of that same yellow rose bush.

Among all ather's political enemies, there was no one whom he hated so cordially as General Benjamin F. Butler[2]. He could never think of enough bad things to say about "old Ben Butler." It was June a year or two after the "proselytizing" of Mother. The yellow rose bush was again in its glory. One morning in a fine turn out, a barouche[3] drawn by a handsome pair of grays, stopped in the road before the house. The driver on his high seat motioned for Father to approach. There was no mistaking that much caricatured figure on the back seat, the huge flat topped head, the dropping eyelid, the sinister mouth. But General Butler as affable and smiling that morning. "Would the gentleman kindly give me some of those beautiful yellow roses?" The gentleman would. And in an instant Father was striding toward the rose bush, opening his jack knife. He cut and cut, and carried a great armful to lay in General Butler's lap. Then followed a happy talk about crops, and the beauty of Pleasant Valley, and then the carriage drove on. Sheepishly Father returned to the house and smiling Mother said, "I expect we shall see you voting for Ben Butler for governor this fall." I don't think Father ever did vote for General Butler but his shafts where broken. Meekly he took his medicine from Mother's caustic spoon.

IX. In War Time

One of the vivid recollections of my very early boyhood, is of standing one evening with the whole family under the great Balms of Gilead tree in front of the house, to gaze up through a rift in the foliage, at a comet blazing out against the blue back of the autumn sky. My astronomy tells me it was in October 1858, and that the name of the blazing stranger was Donati's Comet[1]. Donati was an Italian astronomer who was appointed assistant in 1852 at the observatory in Florence. There he discovered, in addition to five others, the brilliant comet of 1858. We watched it for several evenings, changing its position each night with reference to the tree, growing dimmer and dimmer until it disappeared from sight. I do not think we were a superstitious people yet I am sure that many older ones shared the small boy's relief when the fiery stranger was seen no more. In 1858, no man needed the baleful light of Donati's Comet to enable him to read in the signs of the times the coming of war.

In the autumn of 1860 came the most momentous presidential campaign in American history. The one absorbing issue was negro slavery. The old Democratic Party, of which Father was a lifelong follower, was divided. The new Republican Party with it Abolitionist principles, gained the ascendancy and elected Abraham Lincoln as President. Great was Father's discontent. He sincerely believed, as did a great many others, that Lincoln was an utter incompetent. "Old Abe is honest but he don't know much," was his oft repeated remark. Reviled, misrepresented, a misunderstood, the brave, the patient wide man in the White House went his unswerving way. The slow change in my Father's mind, the growing confidence in Lincoln which even a small boy could discern, as the war dragged on, was the steady crystallizing conviction of the whole nation.

How much of the significance of the historic march of events of those four years, a boy from eight to twelve years of age could grasp and how much is the impression of subsequent reading, I find hard to determine. My memory of those years is very vivid.

At noon on the 15th of April 1861, my Father came home from the city with the astounding, crushing news that Fort Sumpter had surrendered, and that President Lincoln was about to issue a call for seventy-five thousand volunteers to put down the rebellion. The long roll of the drum beat of the nation that April day was heard and heeded in Pleasant Valley. All over the north, before the sun went down that night, was the sound of marching feet. Within forty-eight hours after the President's call the old Sixth Regiment of Massachusetts[2], ranks full, every man armed and equipped, was marching southward swelling the nations song, "We're coming, Father Abraham, a hundred thousand strong", and Pleasant Valley was in step with it all.

It was on Tuesday or Wednesday morning of that week that, by a stone post at the corner[3] of Essex and Broadway in Lawrence, I sat astride my Father's shoulders and saw the soldiers march by, to the station to entrain for Boston. It was all very wonderful to me, the stirring music of the band.

In the lead, the long procession of escorting citizens, the shouting multitudes along the street. Just as the close ranks of the company came opposite us, my uncle, in his handsome uniform, recognized us, smiled, nodded, and waved his sword.

And so, we sent forth our first offering. How many times that scene of parting with our soldier boys at the station was to be repeated, few of us had any idea. The Sixth regiment was enlisted for three months. The opinion was quite generally expressed, that before the expiration of that time, we should welcome our soldiers home again, the rebellion put down, the rebels fitly punished. But in three months came the crushing, humiliating defeat of Bull Run. We then saw the true nature of war. It was to be a fight to the finish with a brave people, American's of the same blood as ourselves.

On the post at the corner of Mother's garden, we fastened a box in which the milkman, as he returned from the market each morning, placed a daily paper, for the weekly was quite insufficient. In the evening, we all assembled in the living room, where Mother, in a clear voice that never tired, read to us all the news columns of *the Boston Herald*[1].

A war map of the southern states was purchased, and hung on the east side of the living room, where it reached from the ceiling almost to the floor. The few battles that had already been fought were marked by red dots. We all constantly studied that map. By standing on the old lounge, before it I could intelligently follow the movements of armies and navies on land and sea. I was provided with a red pencil to locate the new battlefields. How the red spots dotted every part of the map as the slow campaigns moved along - Wilson's creek, Shiloh, Vicksburg, Fair Oaks, Chicamauga. How those red spots told of the suffering of the North, the dying of the South. My pencil marched with Sherman from Atlanta to the sea. Standing on a box on the old lounge, I reached up to the place the red spot on Gettysburg. As if it were but yesterday, I recall the agony which we followed the life and death struggle of those to great armies billowing across the red field of Gettysburg those three hot July days.

I am sure that the education of those evenings in the living room, made us all more ardent patriots. My patriotism found expression in a boy's way, I had my flag and nailed it to a mast by the mail box ,where it waved throughout storm and sunshine, victory and defeat, growing frayed and faded as the years went by. A soldier in uniform was an idol in my eyes. White stripes sewed on the outer seams of my blue denim trousers and a soldier's cap helped to express my military ardor.

The short-trousered patriots of the Valley, organized a military company of home guards. I had hoped to be an officer but the possession of a wooden gun, painted to look just like a real one, kept me in the ranks. Later the gift of a fife[5] transferred me to the band. We marched and drilled many hours. One Saturday afternoon we marched with full ranks to the top of Webster's Hill, where we attached a strongly entrenched army of rebels under command of General Lee. The Rebs resisted strongly, but a splendid charge we dislodged them and drove them into the woods and marched home without a casualty in season for supper.

This childish soldiering helped us in many ways and perhaps later bore direct fruit. When in the last months of the struggle, the North was drawing itself up that final knock-out blow to the staggering Confederacy, a call came for young men and boys for one hundred days. Then it was that several of the older boys of our company donned the blue uniform and had some modest share in the great closing events.

As the years wore on and the strain and suspense reached almost the breaking point, old and young found relief in the occasional Sunday evening gatherings at the schoolhouse. A few brief prayers would be offered from burdened hearts. The singing of patriotic songs gave renewed courage to us all.

"Rally round the flag boys,
Rally once again,
Shouting the battle cry of Freedom
John Brown's body lies mouldering in the grave
As we go marching on."[6]

How we roared out those soulful songs. Sometimes in an interval of waiting silence some tired woman's tremulous voice would start that restful old Methodist hymn;

"In the sweet fields of Eden
Where the tree of Life is a blooming,
There is rest for the weary,
There is rest for you."[7]

These songs rehearsed at the Sunday evening meetings at the school house were taken home and sung alone in the kitchen, in the furrow an at the wood pile. I recall as but yesterday a summer morning just before haying in 1864. We were at work in the lower field by the river. The June sunshine flashed on the blue river, the June breeze billowed the tall grass, the bobolinks darted across the field with little explosions of rippling song as though there were no war. On the other side of the field Father was ploughing with Pony and singing with a touch of pathos in his rich voice;

"We're tenting tonight on the old camp ground
Many are the hearts that are weary tonight
Waiting for the war to cease."[8]

Another vivid memory of those years is of the sound of the bells of the city coming to us through the still evening air. It is one of the traditions of the city of Lawrence, that in the early days it was left to General Henry K. Oliver, a distinguished musician, the author of that grand old tune "Federal Street," to determine what should be the tone of every new bell hung in the mills and steeples of the city. In time, Lawrence possessed a sort of wide spread carillon of harmonizing bells. It became the custom during the war, to ring the bells of the city at sunset to announce a great battle, whether a victory or defeat for our army. And we, sitting on the front door step in the cool still evening, would listen to the sweetly blending sounds of many bells and wait, between hope and fear, for the coming of the morning paper. Had we known Tennyson in those days someone would have quoted:

> "Ring out the old, ring in the new
> Ring out the false, ring in the true.[9]"

The war brought many changes into our daily life. War prices, while they helped us in disposing of the products of the farm, incited our innate economy to dire parsimony. We never bought anything the farm could produce, nor anything for which the farm could provide any sort of substitute. An orange was to me a sick-room luxury. I never heard of a banana, until I found the word translating "*Paul and Virginia*"[10] and brought one to see what it was like. For the coffee, we roasted grains of rye and barley. We came to know that "crust coffee," made from roasted crusts of brown bread, was not unpalatable[11].

The blockade of southern ports made cotton goods very scarce. Every shred of old cotton cloth to be found, Mother and Sister washed and took away in bundles to a neighbor's where the women of the Valley spent many afternoons scraping lint and rolling bandages for the Sanitary Commission.

When dyestuffs became hard to obtain, Mother sent me to gather lichens from the rocks along the pasture walls. From such growths steeped a long time she made, with alum mordants[12], dyes of many delicate shades of yellow, orange, and pale green.

In the absence of hunters roaming through the autumn woods, small game became plentiful. In the woods at the top of our hill, I set long lines of snares. I had never been told and never thought, of the cruelty of the practice. What a joy it was, after the morning milking, to start off the visit my traps. I climbed up across the hill pasture in the crisp October air, the Hunter's moon just finishing its long night journey, settling slowly down behind Webster's Hill, the east beginning to brighten with the first rays of the coming day.

Over the tree-tops to the south, I could see the tall factory chimneys belching black smoke[13], in preparation for the long day of weaving the blue army cloth for soldiers' uniforms. By the time I reached the head of my line of snares, the sun was gilding the tree-tops and it was daylight in the woods. It was very exciting to look down the long line and see here, a partridge, beyond, two rabbits and still farther along another partridge dangling on the line added spice and flavor to the excitement. My wild game, carried home in triumph, added not a little to our war scrimped table.

On the afternoon of the fifteenth of April 1865, four years to the very day after the receipt of tiding of the fall of Sumpter, we were harnessing Pony under the Balm of Gilead tree. A stranger who had come up to make some inquiry was just turning back into the road when one of my schoolmates rushed up shouting, "Guess what is the news!" "I guess Johnston has surrendered," I replied. "No, President Lincoln is shot!" Father, who was just stopping and buckling the hame strap[14], turned fiercely upon the boy, "What's that?" The stranger, overhearing, turned back and told us all the terrible story as he had heard it in the city. President Lincoln had been shot the evening before in Ford's theatre and had been carried into the house opposite and there had died at seven o'clock that morning. I can never forget Father's white face, the tears coursing down his cheeks, as he turned and stripped the harness from the horse, forgetting out errand, and muttering, "the South has killed its best friend."

All my life I have been eager for knowledge of Lincoln. Hay and Nicolay's many volume history[15], has never been enough. Twice in my life Mr. Lincoln has seemed very near to me, almost a personal presence. That April afternoon, as we stood beneath the old Gilead tree and heard the story of the martyrdom from the stranger's lips and I saw Father's deep grief for the man, whom four years before he had so despised, Mr. Lincoln seemed very near to me.

One February twelfth, just before the Great War, I was to speak on Lincoln at Cooper Union[16] in New York City. The old caretaker of the hall, who had seen and heard Lincoln speak there, brought out for my use the chair in which he had sat and, with a piece of chalk, marked the precise spot on which Lincoln had stood to deliver the famous Cooper Union Speech[17] that made him President. As I stood on that sacred spot to tell a great audience of men and boys, of every nation under the sun, much of his humble early life, more of his freeing the slave, most of his saving and restoring a broken Union for them, Americans to be, for the second time Abraham Lincoln seemed very near to me, almost a personal presence.

The war was over. Pleasant Valley had done her part, had given of her finest, and best. From one family had gone three stalwart sons. There was no bullet cast that could harm them, but in camp they all contracted tuberculosis. They came home to die the slow, lingering death of that disease in the arms of their agonized parents. From another home went a father and two sons[18], the younger a boy of fifteen or sixteen years, a drummer boy in his father's company. That drummer boy came home at the end of the war the colonel of his regiment.[19]

As I read of a whole world in chaos every since the Great War, I recall home not much aged in heart, only a little graver and maturer. The next day we saw them at the plough handles, thriftily getting a little more wear out of the faded blue uniforms.

X. Thanksgiving

We gave no thought to Christmas in the early years. Thanksgiving[1] is naturally the great festival of the farm. At that time, the thoughts of all the absentees of New England birth turn longingly to the old home farm. Our preparation for the great day began at least two weeks before, with the butchering, a dreadful ordeal but without which there would be no meat for the mince pies[2].

For several days after the butchering, we kept the brass kettles hanging over the open fire, boiling down cider[3]. All day and far into the night we filled up and skimmed the steaming kettles of the sweet juice till a barrel was reduced to a few gallons. There is a story that one morning the great divine, Lyman Beecher[4], suddenly appeared in the kitchen of the parsonage at Litchfield, in the midst of the bustle of the Saturday baking, his quill pen behind his ear, something weighty on his mind. Gaining the attention of the chief cook we said, "Wife, I have been thinking that this year we ought to put down two barrels of boiled cider apple sauce[5] instead of the barrel and a half of last year." Having thus relieved his mind the famous preacher went back to his study and his sermon. Often times we surpassed the best output of the Litchfield kitchen. All winter, cider apple sauce was on the table at very meal.

While the cider simmers over the fire, let me tell you of the barrel of juice that was boiled down without any fire. Once we brought home a barrel from the mill, set it up on the skids in the cellar and left it without removing the bung, as we had intended to boil it down the next day. But several days passed before we could again take thought of the barrel. By that time we feared that it had begun to work so, lighting the lantern, we went down cellar to investigate. The first thing was to remove the bung, Father, standing over the barrel, began to tap with a hammer on the barrel each side of the bung, but the bung stuck and the taps increased to blows. Then something happened. The heavy bung was hurled with terrific force straight up within an inch of Father's nose, knocking off his hat and bringing a loose shelf above clattering down on his head while a geyser of frothing cider erupted into his face. It was all too much for me. I dropped to the floor and rolled and roared with the most unfilial laughter. Father, bareheaded, his wet face dripping, turned on me with deserved rage, "Laugh will ye. That damned cannon ball most knocked my head off. I s'pose you'd laugh if you had killed me. Now laugh till you split." The barrel of cider was nearly half boiled away by that eruption. The rest we poured into the vinegar barrel.[6]

For two evenings, at least we chopped the meat, the suet and the apples, for Mother always planned to have laid in ordered rows on the buttery shelves, a hundred mince pies. There was a keen rivalry in our valley, as to who should made the best mince pie. The arbiter of the merit of the pies was a venerable, slow spoken, dear old deacon. It was sometimes said that the good deacon, a strong temperance advocate, awarded the palm to the pie containing the most brandy. Of course it wasn't true. But Mother always drew the line at boiled cider.

A large company on Thanksgiving Day sat down at the two or three tables spread in the living room. Carefully it was planned that at no table should be seated thirteen guests. And how those tables were loaded! The turkey on the largest platter, lay before Father flanked by two plump chickens on either side. There was every vegetable the garden could furnish. At every plate were dishes of cranberry and apple-sauce. At the ends of each table stood big dishes of shining apples chinked in with walnuts, chestnuts, and raisins. After the meats came plum pudding[7], followed by fruit-cake[8]. Last were served the pies, to each guest a generous wedge of mince, apple[9], pumpkin[10] and cranberry pie[11]. Cider was never forgotten. Before we sat down, Father filled the goblets from several pitchers, carefully adapting the beverage to the age and taste of each guest, from the sweet juice just from the mill, to old cider hard as rocks.

And when Father is sure every one is stuffed to capacity, he pushes back his chair and says, "Now let's go for a walk to settle out dinner." With glad alacrity we all bustle up from the table to obey the summons. We always take just the same walk. We flock out across the hill pasture, stopping a few minutes under the big chestnut tree, to hunt for nuts among the burrs, then on up the hill, the little groups drawn together by the eternal affinity of love and friendship, to the top. And there, we stand and look down over Pleasant Valley alight in the sunshine of the brief November afternoon, the blue river bending round the hill, the white winged gulls circle above the island in the distance, Father leaning on his cane a little more each year, Mother in her talk a little more inclined to the backward look and reminiscences of earlier Thanksgiving days.

Of all the goodly company I alone remain. Alone I sit down at the table of memory. No, no, not alone, for with me is the dear companion who has walked by my side almost fifty years. I hear the merry voices of children and grandchildren and the greetings of an ever widening circle of dear and faithful friends.

> "Grow old along with me
> The best is yet to be,
> The last of life, for which the first was made."[12]

Endnotes

Chapter I: Pleasant Valley

1. Gage's Ferry: one of five ferries over the Merrimack River. The Andover Bridge (Broadway/Londonderry Turnpike) replaced the Ferry system.

2. Cross' 'four corners' in front of his house is now the intersection of Pleasant Valley St (Rt. 113) with Merrimack St (Rt. 110) and Ferry road, in Methuen, Mass.

3. Lawrence Road is now Merrimack Street.

4. The Samuel Cross, Jr. House stood at 369 Merrimack Street Methuen. The Simeonian's, a farming family from Armenia purchased it and continued farming for many years. Later in the 20th century the homestead was used as a hotel. The site has a small business building there now.

5. The two story Pleasant Valley School still exists and is now a day care.

6. tarvia: a viscid surfacing and binding material for roads that is made from coal tar

7. Samuel Cross, Jr. [b. Feb 28 1811] was the son of Samuel and Abigail Cross; married Lydia Whittier Frye [b. Nov 10, 1816] on Aug 27, 1837 and had several surviving children: Edward Whittier Cross b. Sept 19, 1839, Hannah Jennie Cross b. 1844, and George Newton Cross b .1853 - 1930.

8. Webster's Hill: this hill occupies the area between Merrimack River and Rt 110, it is now occupied by single family homes.

9. Mitchell's Falls: located on the west side of the oxbow in the Merrimack between Lawrence, Methuen and Haverhill, Mass. One of the two significant falls, out of six, not flooded out by the construction of the Great Stone Dam at Bodwell's Falls; while still an impediment to

navigation, it no longer qualifies as a waterfall, and is now a minor rapid.

10. town crier or bellman: an officer of the court who makes public pronouncements as required by the court. The crier can also be used to make public announcements in the streets. Criers often dress elaborately, by a tradition dating to the 18th century, in a red and gold robe, white breeches, black boots and a tricorne hat. They carry a handbell to attract people's attention, as they shout the words "Oyez, Oyez, Oyez!" before making their announcements. The word "Oyez" means "hear ye," which is a call for silence and attention. Oyez derives from the Anglo-Norman word for listen.

11. shoemaking: before intense centralization of factories, many Methuen farmers and workers of all stripes, brought shoe-making piecework material home to make shoes during their off hours, especially in winter.

12. twenty-five cents had the relative value of 5.00 USD in today's economy.

13. one dollar would have had the relative value of 26.00 USD in today's economy.

Chapter II: The Old Home

1. George's Mother Lydia Whittier Frye Cross.

2. rhubarb (pie weed) - from *Practical American Cookery and Domestic Economy.* by E M Hall. New York: Auburn, Miller, Orton & Mulligan, (1856) – "Cut the large stalks off where the leaves commence; strip off the outside skin; then cut the stalk in pieces half an inch long; line a pie dish with paste, rolled rather thicker than a dollar piece; put in a layer of the rhubarb, nearly an inch deep; to a quart bowl of cut rhubarb, put a large teacup of sugar; strew it over, with a salt spoon full of salt, and half a nutmeg, grated ; cover with a rich pie crust; cut a slit in the center; trim off the edge with a sharp knife, and bake in a quick oven, until the pie loosens from the dish."

3. rollway: a place on which things are rolled or moved on rollers; a pile of logs in or at the side of a river or stream ready to go to the mill.

4. thyrsi: a staff tipped with a pine cone and sometimes entwined with ivy or vine leaves

5. whatnot: A set of light, open shelves for ornaments

6. hair wreaths were one of the most popular forms of fancywork, from 1850 to 1875. Hair was manipulated to resemble a variety of flowers, floral sprigs, and leaves, it served as a tangible remembrance friends and family. Hair was also sometimes taken after a person's death as a means of honor and remembrance.

7. Hanah Jennifer Cross b. 1844. in 1870 at 25, Jennie married widower Wm. Sleeper (45), a well to do farmer with 200 acres and three children. When William passed away, Jennie moved in with her step daughter Kate Sleeper Piece and her family in Haverhill.

8. chine: A cut of meat containing part of the backbone.

Chapter III: The Ways of the Household

1 brown bread: from *Practical American cookery and domestic economy* by E M Hall. New York and Auburn, Miller, Orton & Mulligan, (1856) – "A person once accustomed to this bread will never willingly live without it. To make it, take one quart of rye meal, two quarts of Indian meal" if not fresh, scald it with half a teacup full of molasses, two teaspoons full of salt, one teaspoonful of saleratus,* one teacup full of home brewed yeast, or half the quantity of distillery yeast ; make it as stiff as can be stirred with a spoon, with warm water, and let it rise from night till morning. Then put it into a large, deep pan, smooth the top with the hand, dipped in cold water, let it stand a few minutes, and then bake it in an oven five or six hours. If put in late in the day, it may remain in the oven over night." [*Saleratus was a name brand of sodium bicarbonate]

2 Indian pudding: from *Godey Lady's Book* (1863) – "Two quarts of boiling water, with Indian meal enough to make a thin batter; stir in while boiling hot. Add sugar, allspice to your taste; also a teacup of cold milk. Bake five hours in a moderate oven."

3. Rob Roy, the Scottish folk hero reputedly used caves to hide in during various times when cattle rustling.

4. baked beans: from *The New England cook book, or Young housekeeper's guide.* New Haven, Conn.:Herrick and Noyes (1836) – "Pick over the beans, wash, and put them in a pot with cold water enough to cover them, hang them over the fire where they will keep just lukewarm. When they begin to grow soft, stew them over a hot fire several minutes, with a heaping teaspoonful of saleratus*. Then take them up with a skimmer, and put them in a baking pot, gash a lb.

of pork and put it down in the pot so as to have the beans just cover it, pour in cold water till you can see it at the top. They will bake in a hot oven in the course of three hours; but they will be better to remain in it five or six. Beans are very good stewed, without being baked." [*Saleratus was a name brand of sodium bicarbonate]

5. pan dowdy: from *Good Housekeeping (*1888) – "Half fill a baking dish with sliced apples, and cover with butter. Mix together one pint of flour, one-fourth of a cupful of sugar, one half of a teaspoon of salt, one large teaspoonful of baking powder, add one cupful of milk, one egg, two teaspoonfuls of butter melted in two tablespoons of boiling water. Bake and serve with sauce."

6. Villa Trollope (Villino Trollope), for twenty years, before being converted into and converted into an American 'pension' or a resting place for travelers, it was the residence of historian and writer Thomas Adolphus Trollope, an older brother of Anthony Trollope. He produced some sixty volumes of travel writing, history and fiction, in addition to a large amount of periodical and journalistic work. His second wife Frances Trollope. was the author of the satire "*Domestic Manners of the Americans*."

7. doughnut: from *Miss Beecher's Domestic Receipt Book: Designed as a Supplement Treatise On Domestic Economy*. New York: Harper & Brothers, 1846 – "One pound of butter. One pound and three quarters of sugar, worked with the butter. Three pints of milk. Four eggs. One pint of yeast, if home-made, or half a pint of distillery yeast. Mace and cinnamon to the taste. Flour enough to make the dough stiff as biscuit. Rub the butter and sugar together, add the other ingredients, and set the dough in a warm place to rise. When thoroughly light, roll into sheets, cut with a sharp knife into diamond-shaped pieces, and boil them in fresh lard. Use a good deal of lard, and have it sufficiently hot, or the cake will absorb the fat."

8. Uncle Hiram – *[unknown reference as of Sept. 2012 - ed.]*

9. cranberry turnovers (fried pies): from *The Young Housekeeper's Friend; or, A Guide to Domestic Economy and Comfort* by Mary Hooker Cornelius. Boston, C. Tappan; New York, Saxton & Huntington, (1846) – Fried Apple Pie. "Roll out light bread dough, lay on little bits of butter, and fold it up, just as for pastry. This done once will do very well , especially if the bread is made of milk. Then roll out pieces of it very thing, in an oblong shape, and lay upon one half each, apple which is stewed and seasoned to your taste. It should not be very juicy, nor be laid very near the edge of the crust. Wet the edge at least an inch wide, and sprinkle it with flour, as in making fruit

pies; turn the other half of the crust over the apple, and press the edge down so as to close it entirely, else the fat will fill the inside. Fry it precisely like doughnuts, only twice as long. The crust should be rolled very thing, or else it will be difficult to cook it through, on account of the moisture of the apple."

10. *Godey's Magazine and Lady's Book,* was the most widely circulated magazine in the period before the Civil War. Each issue contained poetry, articles, and engravings created by prominent writers and other artists of the time. Sarah Josepha Hale (author of "Mary Had a Little Lamb") was its editor from 1837 until 1877 and only published original, American manuscripts. Although the magazine was read and contained work by both men and women, Hale published three special issues which only included work done by women. When Hale started at Godey's, the magazine had a circulation of ten thousand subscribers. Two years later, it jumped to 40,000 and by 1860 had 150,000 subscribers.

11. *The History of the Decline and Fall of the Roman Empire* is a six volume history book by English historian Edward Gibbon, covering the history of the Roman Empire, Europe, and the Catholic Church from 98 to 1590 and discusses the decline of the Roman Empire in the East and West. Because of its relative objectivity and heavy use of primary sources, at the time, its methodology became a model for later historians.

12. John P. Squire & Company Corporation, a slaughterhouse established 1855 in East Cambridge.

13. Beach Soap Company established 1846 in Lawrence, Mass.

Chapter IV: Ways of the Farm

1. On March 15, 1697, Hannah Duston and some 39 settlers in Haverhill were attacked by the Abenaki Indians. The Indians kidnapped Duston and killed her baby daughter. Duston was held with several others on an island at the confluence of the Merrimack and Contoocook rivers near Concord, N.H. On the night of March 30, the trio escaped. Before leaving, they killed and scalped 10 Indians (men, women and children) as they slept, using hatchets they had stolen from the Indians. They scuttled all the canoes except one, which they used to paddle downriver through the night. At daybreak, the trio spent the first day in Nashua; then the next night they paddled to Haverhill. Duston recognized Bradley's Mill on the Merrimack River.

2. Bradley's Mill was located in Haverhill, about 50 rods from the river near Creek Brook.

3. girt: to bind or encircle; to measure the girth of something.

4. KJV Ruth 2:17, "So, she gleaned in the field until even, and beat out that she had gleaned: and it was about an ephah of barley."

5. National Prohibition Act (Volstead Act), the Eighteenth Amendment, passed October 28, 1919; repealed by the Twenty-first Amendment, adopted December 5, 1933.

6. cider mills were a shared resource; growers would bring their fruit to the mill, and pay for the use of the device with a percentage of the produce.

7. hogshead: a large cask of liquid, a traditional unit of volume for liquids. Originally the hogshead varied with the contents, often being equal to 48 gallons of ale; 54 of beer; 60 of cider; 63 of oil, honey, or wine; or 100 of molasses. In the United States, a hogshead is now defined to hold 2 barrels, or 63 gallons; this was the traditional British wine hogshead.

Chapter V: A Winter Evening in the Living

1. Edward Whittier Cross b. 1839. George's older brother became a teacher himself. He and his wife Martha and their daughter Maude resided in Norfolk, Massachusetts.

2. Fox and Geese: board game where one player is the fox and tries to eat the geese/sheep, and the other player directs the geese/sheep and attempts to trap the fox. The fox is placed in the middle of the board, and 13 geese are placed on one side of the board. The fox and geese can move to any empty space around them (also diagonally). The fox can jump over geese like in checkers, capturing them. Repeated jumps are possible. Geese can not jump. The geese win if they surround the fox so that it cannot move. The fox wins if it captures enough geese that the remaining geese cannot surround it anymore.

3. shoe pegs: Joseph Walker, of Hopkinton, Mass., invented the shoe-peg about 1818, which revolutionized shoe making, prior to that time, all parts of the boot were sewn by hand, but pegging proved to be a great time saver. Before intense centralization of factories, many Methuen farmers and workers of all stripes, brought shoe-making piecework material home to make shoes during their off hours, especially in winter.

4. Seine fishing (or seine-haul fishing): a method of fishing that employs a seine or dragnet. A seine is a fishing net that hangs vertically in the water with its bottom edge held down by weights and its top edge buoyed by floats. Seine nets can be deployed from the shore as a beach seine, or from a boat.

5. Gerrymander: coined by Boston Gazette on March 26, 1812, in reaction to a redrawing of Massachusetts state senate election districts under the then-governor Elbridge Gerry to benefit his political party. When mapped, one of the contorted districts in the Boston area was said to resemble the shape of a salamander.

6. Weary Willie: one who dislikes or avoids work.

7. Cremona, Italy was renowned as a centre of musical instrument manufacture from the 16th century onwards, beginning with the violins of the Amati family, and later included the products of the Guarneri and Stradivari shops. To the present day, their work is widely considered to be the summit of achievement in string instrument making. Cremona is still renowned for producing high-quality instruments.

Chapter VI: In School Days

1. From the poem "In School-Days" by John Greenleaf Whittier.

2. ferule: a rod, cane, or flat piece of wood for punishing children, especially by striking them on the hand.

3. George N. Cross's wife, Mary Sophia Sawyer, 1854-1936; her parents: Alanson Mason Sawyer (1825 - 1895) and Caroline Rollston (Noyes) Sawyer (1830 - 1916) one son: Harold N. Cross (1881 - 1954)

4 buskin: a calf or knee length boot.

5. Hook Sticks: most likely field hockey, which was being played in English public schools in the early 19th century.

6. Old Cat: a 19th century bat-and-ball, safe haven game, numbered according to the number of bases and players. Three Old Cat had a triangular base layout and three strikers, while Four Old Cat had four strikers and four bases in a square pattern. Baseball historian Harold Seymour reported that Old Cat games were still being played on the streets and vacant lots of Brooklyn in the 1920s. Albert Spalding suggested that Four Old Cat was the immediate ancestor of town ball, from which baseball evolved.

7. Snap or crack the whip: usually played in small groups either on grass or ice. One player is the "head" of the whip, runs (or skates) around in random directions, while everyone else holds on to the hand of the previous player. The entire "tail" of the whips around, but more force on the end of the tail. The longer the tail, the tighter they have to hold on. As more players fall off, those that have fallen off, try to grab back onto the tail, and move up and gain a more secure position. References to this game go back to the 1890s in England.

8. tyro: a novice or a beginner in learning something.

9. KJV: John 10:1 "Verily, verily, I say unto you, He that entereth not by the door into the sheepfold, but climbeth up some other way, the same is a thief and a robber."

10. Emerson, Frederick. *The North American Arithmetic, part the first for young learners.* Boston: Jenks & Palmer, (1841); *The North American Arithmetic; part second, uniting oral and written exercises, in corresponding chapters*, Glazier, Masters, and Co., (1838)

11. Greenleaf, Benjamin. *The national arithmetic on the inductive system : combining the analytic and synthetic methods forming a complete course of higher arithmetic.* Boston : Robert S. Davis & Co. (1857).

12. Sargent, Epes. *Standard fifth reader: first-class standard reader for public and private schools containing a summary of rules for pronunciation and elocution, numerous exercises for reading and recitation, a new system of references to rules and definitions, and a copious explanatory index.* Boston, Phillips, Sampson and Co. (1854).

13. Analysis and parsing: Analysis of English composition and sentence structure.

14. Thomas Gray's *Elegy Written in a Country Churchyard* (1751)

15. cutter: a lightweight, open, horse-drawn sleigh, introduced in the United States in about 1800. It usually had a single seat that held two people, but some contained a removable second one, and some had a child's seat that folded out when needed; most have gracefully curved runners and decoratively colored bodies.

16. Dr. Stephen Huse. (b. Dec 30, 1799 - d. August 8, 1864) attended Bradford College, and Harvard Medical School; he was actively involved in the community, as early as 1828 he began serving on the town's school committee and even served as town meeting moderator

from time to time. Was instrumental in the design and construction of the Walnut Grove Cemetary where he is buried.

17. The Methuen Census of 1870 shows - John B Smith, age 43, Farm Laborer, born in Virginia. Other southern born, African-Americans listed in that census were, Henry Hall age 30 born in Virginia, and living with him is Abram Ford age 25, born in Maryland, both listed as laborers who could not read nor write.

18. Samuel H. Taylor, LL.D. (1837-1871), born in Londonderry, NH; Phillips Academy President 1838-1871

19. Taylor, Samuel H. *Classical study: its value illustrated by extracts from the writings of eminent scholars.* Andover, Mass: W. F Draper, (1870).

20. Warren Fales Draper (1818-1905), born East Dedham, Massachusetts; Phillips Academy class of 1843; Amherst class of 1847; joined Allen, Morrill, and Wardwell, printers in Andover in 1849; taking over in 1854, publishing more than six hundred volumes by 1887, some of which had very large sales.

21. Harkness, Albert. *Latin Grammar for Schools and Colleges.* D. Appleton and Co. (1864).

22. Albert Harkness (1822–1907) was an American classical scholar and educator, born at Mendon, Massachusetts; He lectured extensively before learned societies, contributed original research papers in philology; and from 1851 published a series of textbooks in Latin studies, some say beginning of a new era in classical Latin studies in America.

23. William G. Goldsmith (1832-1910) born in Andover, attended Phillips Academy; graduated Harvard in 1857; Principal of Punchard Free School (1858-1870); Peabody Instructor in Phillips Academy, 1870. Acting Principal after Dr. Taylor's death, when passed over for Principal, he returned to Punchard, where he remained until his resignation in 1886; Postmaster of Andover from 1886 to 1895; Andover Selectman from 1898 to 1901.

24. William G. Means (1815-94), born in Amherst NH, Treasurer of the Manchester Locomotive Works, retired to Andover; following in Warren Draper's model, presented forty dollars to be awarded for excellence in "original declamation." These prizes were permanently endowed in his will.

25. Fem Sems – 'female seminarians' from Andover Abbot Academy, founded in 1829, was the first incorporated school for girls in New England.

Chapter VII: The Extension Courses of District Number Six.

1. Syzygy (astronomy), a straight line configuration of three celestial bodies

2. Popcorn balls were among the most popular confections in the late nineteenth century. From Haskell, E. F. *The Housekeeper's Encyclopedia of Useful Information for the Housekeeper in All Branches of Cooking and Domestic Economy*. D. Appleton, (1861) – "Boil honey, maple, or other sugar to the great thread; pop corn and stick the corn together in balls with the candy."

3. "Excelsior" is a brief poem written and published in 1841 by Henry Wadsworth Longfellow. The poem describes a young man passing through a town bearing the banner "Excelsior" (translated from Latin as "ever higher", also loosely but more widely as "onward and upward"), ignoring all warnings, climbing higher until inevitably, "lifeless, but beautiful" he is found by the "faithful hound" half-buried in the snow, "still clasping in his hands of ice that banner with the strange device, Excelsior!"

4. "Casabianca" is a poem by British poet Felicia Dorothea Hemans, first published in the New Monthly Magazine for August 1826. The poem commemorates an actual incident that occurred in 1798 during the Battle of the Nile aboard the French ship Orient. The young son Giocante (his age is variously given as ten, twelve and thirteen) of commander Louis de Casabianca remained at his post and perished when the flames caused the magazine to explode. "The boy stood on the burning deck, Whence all but he had fled, The flame that lit the battle's wreck, Shone round him o'er the dead."

5. Blackface: a form of theatrical makeup used in minstrel shows, where performers created a stereotyped caricature of a black person. The practice gained popularity during the 19th century and contributed to the proliferation of stereotypes. By 1848, blackface minstrel shows were the national art of the time, translating formal art such as opera into popular terms for a general audience. Black performers also were performing in blackface makeup; all-black minstrel shows began to proliferate in the 1860s. Blacks could not perform without blackface makeup, regardless of how dark-skinned they were, reinforcing racist stereotypes.

6. "The September Gale" a poem by Oliver Wendell Holmes (1836) - regarding a hurricane Holmes experienced in September 1815, when he was about seven years old. "I'm not a chicken; I have seen Full many a chill September, And though I was a youngster then, That gale I well remember; The day before, my kite-string snapped, And I, my kite pursuing."

7. Maj. Alfred Little gave his first concert at Pantheon Hall, Fisherville, N. H., in March, 1846. It was so successful that he spent of the next few years traveling and giving concerts. Before then, Little had worked for a manufacturer of reed instruments; while there he constructed his melodeon, and instrument was of a form never seen in these days, being a rectangular box of about 36x18 inches, with flat top in which were inserted the keys, round pieces of ivory, arranged in a double row, corresponding to the position of the white and black keys on a piano; the lower part of this instrument was the bellows, which were operated by the left arm of the performer. He was reputedly although crippled, a wonderful performer on the melodeon, an excellent singer, and a talented actor. He was a noted musician all over New England for many years

8. Binding the feet of well born young girls painfully tight to prevent further growth, representing their freedom from manual labor, it resulted in lifelong disabilities. Begun about 1000 A.D. by the 19th century, some 40–50% of Chinese women had bound feet; for upper class women, the figure was almost 100%

9. a melodeon: a cabinet organ, a type of 19th century reed organ with a foot-operated vacuum bellows, and a piano keyboard. Melodeons were manufactured in the United States sometime after 1812 until the Civil War era.

10. democrat wagon: A light, flat bed farm wagon, usually without a top, with a skeleton frame and two or more seats. "Democrat" referred to the availability, inexpensive, easy to handle, wagon to a wide range of people, designed that if it got stuck a single individual could often lift it out by hand.

11. Jacob Abbott (November 14, 1803 - October 31, 1879), an American writer of children's books. His Rollo books, such as *Rollo at Work, Rollo at Play, Rollo in Europe*, etc., are the best known of his writings, having as their chief characters a representative boy and his associates.

Chapter VIII: The Yellow Rose Bush

1. Medford Rum: reputedly the best rum in the United States at the time, distilled by the Lawrence family, in Medford, Mass for many years. In later years, the Lawrence family sold the right to the name Medford Rum, but not the secret of how to make the original recipe.

2. Benjamin Franklin Butler (1818-1893) served in the United States House of Representatives and later served as the 33rd Governor of Massachusetts. In 1868, as a member of the U.S. House of Representatives, Butler had a prominent role in the impeachment of President Andrew Johnson. As Chairman of the House Committee on Reconstruction, Butler authored the Ku Klux Klan Act of 1871, that gave federal authority to prosecute and destroy the Klan in the South. Butler authored, along with Sen. Charles Sumner, the Civil Rights Act of 1875, which gave African American U.S. citizens the right to public accommodation such as hotels, restaurants, lodging, and public entertainment establishments.

3. barouche: a fashionable type of horse-drawn carriage it was a four-wheeled, shallow vehicle with two double seats inside, arranged so that the sitters on the front seat faced those on the back seat. It had a soft collapsible half-hood folding like a bellows over the back seat and a high outside box seat in front for the driver.

Chapter IX: In War Time

1. Donati's Comet, (C/1858 L1 and 1858 VI), is a long-period comet named after the Italian astronomer Giovanni Battista Donati who first observed it on June 2, 1858. After the Great Comet of 1811, it was the most brilliant comet that appeared in the 19th century. It was also the first comet to be photographed. It was nearest the Earth on October 10, 1858. Abraham Lincoln, then a candidate for a seat in the U.S. Senate, sat up on the porch of his hotel in Jonesboro, Illinois to see "Donti's Comet" on September 14, 1858, the night before the third of his historic debates with Stephen Douglas.

2. The Sixth Massachusetts Volunteer Militia formerly organized on January 21, 1861. With war approaching, men who worked in the textile cities of Lowell and Lawrence joined this new infantry regiment. On April 15th, three days after the attack on Fort Sumpter, they shipped out to defend Washington, D.C. When they arrived in the border state of Maryland three days later, an angry mob awaited them. In the riot that followed, 16 people lost their lives. Four were soldiers from

Massachusetts. These men were the first combat fatalities of the Civil War.

3. Railroad station was located near the corner of Essex street and Broadway, in Lawrence, Mass.

4. The Boston Herald is a conservative daily newspaper that serves Boston, Massachusetts, United States, and its surrounding area. It was started in 1846 and is one of the oldest daily newspapers in the United States.

5. Fife: a small, high-pitched, transverse flute that is similar to the piccolo, but louder and shriller due to its narrower bore.

6. "John Brown's Body", an American marching song about the abolitionist John Brown. Popular in the Union during the American Civil War. The song's authorship is disputed, one account claims the lyrics were a collective effort by Union soldiers and that the lyrics also referred humorously to Sergeant John Brown of the Second Battalion, Boston Light Infantry Volunteer Militia. The coarseness and irreverence led many of the era to feel uncomfortable with the earliest "John Brown" lyrics, leading to the creation of many variant versions of the text that aspired to a higher literary quality; most famously Julia Ward Howe's "The Battle Hymn of the Republic."

7. "Rest for the Weary", William Hunter (1857).

8. "Tenting on the Old Camp Ground" was a popular song during the American Civil War. A particular favorite of enlisted men in the Union army, it was written in 1863 by Walter Kittredge and first performed in that year at Old High Rock, Lynn, Massachusetts

9. "Ring Out, Wild Bells" is a poem by Alfred, Lord Tennyson, published in 1850.

10. *Paul et Virginie* (or *Paul and Virginia*) is a novel by Jacques-Henri Bernardin de Saint-Pierre, first published in 1787. The novel's title characters are very good friends since birth who fall in love.

11. Brown bread crust coffee: from *The American Frugal Housewife Dedicated to Those Who Are Not Ashamed of Economy* by Lydia Maria Child (1830) – "Coffee Substitutes: As substitutes for coffee, some use dry brown bread crusts, and roast them; other soak rye grain in rum, and roast it; other roast peas in the same way as coffee. None of these are very good; and peas so used are considered unhealthy. Where there is a large family of apprentices and workmen, the coffee is very dear, it may be worth while to use the substitutes, or

to mix them half and with coffee; but, after all, the best economy is to go without."

12. mordant: a mineral substance used to set dyes on fabrics or tissue sections by forming a coordination complex with the dye which then attaches to the fabric or tissue

13. Lawrence, Mass. was once a large scale factory town, known for miles of brick factories and tall smoke stacks. Unlike, Lowell, Mass. which closed most of its factories, putting 11,000 out of work, Lawrence manufacturers had stockpiled cotton, and had factories that produced woolen textiles.

14. hame strap: connects the right and left hames together on top and bottom. Hames are either of two curved supports that are attached to the collar of a draft horse and that hold the traces.

15. John Nicolay and John Hay, personal secretaries to Abraham Lincoln, published a mammoth ten-volume biography: *Abraham Lincoln: A History in Ten Volumes* (1890)

16. Cooper Union for the Advancement of Science and Art, founded in 1859 and commonly referred to simply as Cooper Union, is a privately funded college in the East Village neighborhood of Manhattan, New York City, located at Cooper Square and Astor Place.

17. "The Cooper Union Address" was delivered by Abraham Lincoln on February 27, 1860. He was not yet the Republican nominee for the presidency. Considered one of his most important speeches, Lincoln elaborated his views on slavery, affirming that he did not wish it to be expanded into the western territories and claiming that the Founding Fathers would agree with this position. Horace Greeley's New York Tribune hailed it as "one of the most happiest and most convincing political arguments ever made in this City ... No man ever made such an impression on his first appeal to a New-York audience."

18. Leverett Bradley (1814-1880), Captain Company B, First Regiment of Heavy Artillery Massachusetts Volunteers; his sons, Leverett Bradley, Jr (1846-1902) age 16 at enlistment October 1861, mustered out first lieut. in 1865. Jeremiah (Jerry) Payson Bradley, enlisted as bugler at age 14 in 1861 his service expired in '64 still a musician.

19. Jerry P. Bradley, entered the state militia in 1873, he became adjutant with the rank of first lieutenant in the First Battalion of Cavalry; was appointed by Gov. Wolcott, in 1897, assistant adjutant general with the rank of colonel and served three years, including the Spanish war period.

Chapter X: Thanksgiving

1. Thanksgiving: Although George Washington proclaimed the first nation-wide thanksgiving celebration in America on November 26, 1789, "as a day of public thanksgiving", and by the mid 19th century many states celebrated it by gubernatorial proclamation, it was Sarah Josepha Hale, editor of *Godey's Lady's Book*, who is the "Mother of the American Thanksgiving". In 1846, Hale began an editorial campaign to make Thanksgiving a national holiday. In 1863, in the midst of America's Civil War, President Abraham Lincoln proclaimed the first annual national Thanksgiving.

2. mince meat pie: from *The American Practical Cookery-Book by A Practical Housekeeper*. Philadelphia: J.W. Bradley, (1860) -"Three pounds of tender lean beef, a pound and a half of suet, half as much prepared apple as meat, two pounds of chopped raisins stoned, two pounds clean currants, two pounds sugar, two cups molasses, one gill rose-water, the rind and juice of four lemons, one pint of wine or brandy, salt, mace, cloves, cinnamon, black pepper, ginger, two tablespoon-fuls extract vanilla. Chop the meat, suet and apples, very fine. Add to them the raisins and currants. Then dissolve the sugar in the brandy, and mix thoroughly together all the remaining ingredients. Fill a deep plate with a rich paste; fill, cover and bake. Mince pies are always made with covers, and should be eaten warm."

3. Boiled cider: cider which has been slowly boiled over a low flame, until it becomes the consistency of syrup. "Heat on medium-low for several hours, simmer, stirring occasionally until it has reduced by about 80%- 85%."

4. Lyman Beecher (1775-1863) notable New England minister, American Temperance Society co-founder, the father of 13 children, many of whom became noted figures, including Harriet Beecher Stowe, Henry Ward Beecher.

5. boiled cider sweetened apple sauce: from *The New England cook book, or Young housekeeper's guide.* New Haven, Conn.:Herrick and Noyes, (1836) - Apple Sauce: "Pare and quarter the apples, take out the cores, stew them in cider. When soft take them up, put in a piece of butter of the size of a walnut, to every quart of the sauce, sweeten it to your taste, with brown sugar. Another way which is very good, is to boil the apples, with a few quinces, in new cider, and molasses enough to sweeten them, till reduced to half the quantity. This kind of sauce will keep good for several months."

6. Vinegar made from apple cider or apple must has a pale to medium amber color. When unpasteurized it contains "mother of vinegar", a substance composed of a form of cellulose and acetic acid bacteria which turns alcohol into acetic acid with the help of oxygen from the air. The "mother" has a cobweb-like appearance and can make the vinegar look slightly congealed. As the vinegar is used from the barrel, more cider is added to the mother, which creates more vinegar.

7. plum pudding: from *Practical American cookery and domestic economy* by E M Hall. New York and Auburn, Miller, Orton & Mulligan, (1856) – "Half a pound of raisins, half a pound of currants, half a pound of bread, grated, half a pound of apples, chopped, four eggs, half a nutmeg, a wine-glass of brandy, a quarter of a pound of suet. Boil three hours."

8. fruit cake: from *Practical American cookery and domestic economy* by E M Hall. New York and Auburn, Miller, Orton & Mulligan, (1856) – "One pound of flour, one pound of sugar, three-quarters of a pound of butter, and ten eggs. First beat the yolks and sugar together, then add the flour and butter, beaten to a cream; and lastly, mix in lightly the whites of the eggs, beaten to a high froth. Stone and chop one or two pounds of raisins, (as you may choose,) two pounds of currants, well cleaned and dried, one of citron, a quarter of a pound of almonds, half an ounce of mace, a teaspoon full of rosewater, a wine-glass of brandy, and one of wine ; stir in the flour gradually, then the wine, brandy, and spice. Add the fruit just before it is put into the pans. It takes over two hours to bake it if the loaves are thick ; if the loaves are thin, it will bake in less time. This kind of cake is the best after it has been made three or four weeks, and it will keep good five or six months."

9. apple pie: from *The New England cook book, or Young housekeeper's guide.* New Haven, Conn.: Herrick and Noyes, (1836) – "Pare, quarter, and take out the cores of the apples, and if not ripe, stew them before baking them, and season them to your taste. Butter your plates, put on a thin under crust, fill the plates, and cover them with a thick crust. Bake them about three quarters of an hour. When done take off the upper crust carefully, and put a piece of butter of the size of a walnut, into each pie, sweeten them to your taste, if not acid enough, squeeze in the juice of part of a lemon, or put in a little tartaric acid, dissolved in a little water. Essence of lemon, nutmeg, or rosewater, are all good spice for apple pies. Apples stewed in new cider, and molasses, with a few quinces and strained, with a little cinnamon in it makes nice pies. Dried apples for pies, should have boiling water turned on them, and stewed till tender, then add a little

sour cider, and a little orange peel, and stew them a few moments longer, take them up, put in a little butter, sugar and the juice and peel of a lemon improve them, they are better for being rubbed through a sieve. Fill your pie plates and bake the pies half an hour."

10. pumpkin pie: from *The New England cook book, or Young housekeeper's guide.* New Haven, Conn.: Herrick and Noyes, (1836) – "Cut your pumpkin in two, take out the seeds, and wash the pumpkin, cut it into small strips, and boil it in just water enough to prevent its burning, when tender turn off the water, and let it steam over a moderate fire for fifteen minutes, taking care it does not burn. Take it up, strain it through the sieve, and if you like the pies very thin, put two quarts of milk, to a quart of the pumpkin, and six eggs; if you wish to have them thick, put a quart only of milk, to a quart of pumpkin, and three eggs. Three eggs to a quart of milk does very well, but they are better with five or six. Sweeten it with molasses or sugar, put in ginger, or grated lemon peel to your taste. Bake them in deep plates from fifty to sixty minutes in a hot oven."

11. cranberry pie: from *Practical American Cookery and Domestic Economy* by E M Hall. New York and Auburn, Miller, Orton & Mulligan, (1856) – "Pick a quart of cranberries, free from imperfections; put a pint of water to them, and put them in a stew pan, over a moderate fire ; put a pound of clean brown sugar to them, and stew them gently until they are all soft ; mash them with a silver spoon, and turn them into a dish, to become cold ; then make them into pies or tarts, and bake. Many persons put flour in cranberry pies; it is a great mistake, as it completely spoils the color of the fruit."

12. apple cider - According to the Massachusetts Department of Agricultural Resources, "Apple juice and apple cider are both fruit beverages made from apples, but there is a difference between the two. Fresh cider is raw apple juice that has not undergone a filtration process to remove coarse particles of pulp or sediment. Apple juice is juice that has been filtered to remove solids and pasteurized so that it will stay fresh longer. V acuum sealing and additional filtering extend the shelf life of the juice."

13. "Rabbi ben Ezra" is a poem by Robert Browning (1812-1888) about Abraham ibn Ezra (1092-1167), one of the great poets, mathematicians and scholars of the 12th century. He wrote on grammar, astronomy, the astrolabe, etc.; published in Browning's *Dramatis Personae* in 1864.

Index

A

B

C

D

E

F

G

H

S

T

U

V

W

Y